LIVING BEYOND
OUR FEARS

ALSO BY BRUCE LARSON

The Presence
A Call to Holy Living
Faith for the Journey
My Creator, My Friend
Wind and Fire
Communicator's Commentary: Luke
Believe and Belong
There's a Lot More to Health Than Not Being Sick
Dare to Live Now
Living on the Growing Edge
No Longer Strangers
The One and Only You
Thirty Days to a New You
Risky Christianity
The Meaning and Mystery of Being Human
Setting Men Free
The Emerging Church
Ask Me to Dance

With J. Keith Miller:

The Edge of Adventure
Living the Adventure
The Passionate People: Carriers of the Spirit

LIVING BEYOND OUR FEARS

Discovering Life When You're Scared to Death

BRUCE LARSON

1817

HARPER & ROW, PUBLISHERS, SAN FRANCISCO
New York, Grand Rapids, Philadelphia, St. Louis
London, Singapore, Sydney, Tokyo, Toronto

FIRST EDITION

Library of Congress Cataloging-in-Publication Data

Larson, Bruce.
    Living beyond our fears: When Love Really Is Enough / Bruce Larson. — 1st ed.
            p.   cm.
      ISBN 0-06-064954-2
      1. Fear—Religious aspects—Christianity. 2. Love—Religious aspects—Christianity.   I. Title.
BV4908.5.L37 1990
241'.4—dc20   89-46022
                                                                                            CIP

90 91 92 93 94 10 HAD 9 8 7 6 5 4 3 2 1

To my wife, known to our grandchildren as "Ace," who not only collaborates on all that I write, but who has collaborated on and edited my journey of faith over these many years, and who holds me when I feel afraid.

CONTENTS

FOREWORD

If you were to tell me your primary fears and your strategies for dealing with those fears, I could tell you a great deal about yourself. Our fears are a psychological and spiritual barometer of who we are. Our personalities are shaped by how we deal with them.

Fear is powerful and elemental, and often irrational. There is healthy fear, such as our fear of poisonous snakes. There is the neurotic fear of the hypochondriac, which can eventually produce illness and even death. There is fear based on truth, such as the fear that cigarette smoking can be hazardous to your health. There is fear based on lies, on misinformation, on gossip, or on old injunctions from dysfunctional parents. Fears can be internal or external, natural or unnatural, focused or unfocused. The list goes on.

Psychologists tell us that when fear erupts, the body is programmed to choose between fight or flight. But in many situations, neither of those options turns out to be relevant or helpful. Researchers also tell us that the worst possible way to deal with fear is to avoid the frightening and to choose a life of inordinate safety and insulation: such a course leads inevitably to psychic and spiritual death. But Americans in alarming numbers are attempting to avoid the fearful through drugs or alcohol: some substance that will dull the pain and quiet the fear, at least temporarily.

In this book, I am working on the bold assumption that there are only two basic emotions: *love and fear.* The Bible tells us that perfect love casts out fear. That's what happens when love and fear meet head-on. A life without fear may not be possible or even desirable, but if God is love, and we can appropriate that love, then a life beyond fear is within our grasp.

I. THE LANDSCAPE OF OUR FEARS

1. Living Beyond Fear

Parental advice has been a shaping force for most of us over the years. We still remember our parents' oft-repeated injunctions, whether or not we follow them. I was urged to work hard and save my money, as were a good many men and women of my generation. A steady job was considered the highest good and Education was stressed as a ticket to a better life. Those of us with Christian parents can remember advice about morality, ethics, and righteousness: be good, keep the Ten Commandments, practice the Golden Rule. My mother spoke to me often about tithing, with a practical approach. "If you give the Lord his portion, he will take good care of you." Another frequent command was to eat everything on my plate. So I was, early on, a fat tither.

That advice passed on by parents was generally an accurate indicator of their own value system, an attempt to transmit their perceptions of what goals and behavior were important. In that light, it is helpful to examine the advice our heavenly Father gives us throughout the Old and New Testaments. It is surprising advice. Oddly enough, it has nothing to do with obedience or morality, at least not directly. The admonition, repeated over and over, is "Fear not."

What timely advice it is! Fear is perhaps our oldest and deadliest enemy. Fear causes illness. It kills. It stifles creativity. Fear prevents love, disrupts families, and causes addiction to alcohol, drugs, work, hobbies, and food. Fear of life and of other people can result in an abnormal desire to withdraw, leading to mental illness. Extreme fear of the future prompts suicide. And yet most of us are seldom free of fear at some level.

From the very beginning, the Bible reiterates this theme of fear. In the third chapter of Genesis, Eve is tempted by the serpent, the Shining One, Satan himself. He convinces her that God is withholding something good from her, that she is being cheated. The fruit of that forbidden tree will make her as wise as God. The serpent is tempting Eve to commit the ultimate sin, which is wanting to be God. Sinful acts, major or minor, from stealing an apple to committing adultery, have their origin in the basic sin, which is unrestrained self-centeredness. I am at the center of the universe, and my family, friends, church, and job are all satellites to my sun.

The first recorded temptation plays on Eve's fear of being cheated. The tempter, then and now, would convince us that God is not our friend. He is actually withholding good things from us. Even after Adam and Eve have disobeyed God, he comes looking for them in the usual place in the garden. Adam, of course, is hiding. Eve and he have covered their nakedness with fig leaves. They know they have broken God's law, and are afraid. The human race has been trying to hide from God ever since. We protect ourselves with defense mechanisms and denials, losing ourselves in destructive habits or obsessive pursuits.

In the very next chapter of Genesis, we meet the first two children of Adam and Eve, Cain and Abel. For some reason unknown to us, Cain's sacrificial offering is not pleasing to God. Cain's fear of God is translated into anger and hatred of his brother, Abel. Fear is often expressed by anger and hostility. Rather than do what is necessary to be reconciled to God, Cain's rage is turned against his brother, and he murders him.

Later in that same book of Genesis, we meet Lot and his family. They have moved into a cave after the destruction of Sodom and Gomorrah, and we are told, "He was afraid to dwell in Zoar." He is fearful about living once again in the city, with its corruption and venal temptations. His is a healthy fear, a fear which prevents him from repeating past calamities. All through the book of Genesis we meet people who have to deal with fear—Hagar, Isaac, Jacob, Rachel, Joseph. From the very beginning of the recorded history of God's people, we find they are fearful people, afraid both of God and of each other.

Fear is universal. It is an emotion all have experienced, from the tribesman in a remote jungle to the sophisticated urbanite. In every age and culture, however, there have been those men and women credited with feats of extraordinary bravery. For the most part, even they claim they were not without fear; rather, they acted in spite of their fears.

Writers and philosophers over the years have reflected on this basic, common emotion. Thousands of years ago, the philosopher Seneca said, "If we let things terrify us, life will not be worth living." In 1840, Thomas Carlyle wrote, "The first duty for a man is still that of subduing fear. A man's acts are slavish until he has got fear under his feet." Thirty years later, Ralph Waldo Emerson remarked that "He has not learned the lesson of life who does not every day surmount a fear." Mark Twain contributed this thought: "The human race is a race of cowards, and I am not only marching in that procession, but I am carrying a banner." Earlier in this century, Ernest Hemingway wrote, "I have always believed that the first duty of a man is still that of subduing fear."

Fear may be universal, but its causes are as varied as our human psyches. Some of us are panicked over money. Do we have enough to take us through the uncertainties of the future? A few years ago, a friend took his retirement money in a lump sum and invested it in the stock market. That black day in October of 1987 wiped him out. I asked him how he was doing. "Actually," he said, "I'm sleeping like a baby. I wake up every three or four hours and cry."

On the other hand, fear is not always a negative emotion. It can serve a useful purpose. Children are taught to fear hot stoves, suspicious strangers, and harmful substances in the medicine chest. There is a lot of healthy fear right now in regard to smoking. What was once considered a harmless habit is now acknowledged to be a deadly addiction, one which causes diseases like lung cancer and emphysema. Men and women are becoming sexually responsible, not because of any commitment to God and his laws, but because promiscuity holds new terrors. A fear of sexually transmitted diseases is forcing society into a more cautious approach to casual relationships. Incidentally, the likelihood of contracting AIDS is higher in the United States than in Haiti. An epidemic has been unleashed primarily as a result of rampant sexual promiscuity.

But whatever our fears, real or imagined, let's keep in mind that fear is the soil where faith grows. One of my favorite verses is "Perfect love casts out fear" (1 John 4:18, RSV). That doesn't mean we are perfect lovers and therefore need not fear. Perfection is not attainable for human beings in this life. Only Jesus is perfect. We are forgiven in and for our imperfections. It is his perfect love, in and through your life and mine, that overcomes fear.

Our fears can act as a barometer, giving us an accurate reading of our true goals and values. Our fears are like the ink blot test psychiatrists administer. The ink blot itself is meaningless, until we give it a meaning by our perception of it.

A *Wall Street Journal* article recently reported on a survey in which men and women from all walks of life were asked, "What is it you fear most?" Contrary to expectations, the fear of death was number three. The fear of failure and the fear of loneliness ranked one and two. A few years ago on retreat with a small group of men, we pursued a variation of that survey question: "What is it you fear worse than death?" Of the seven men present, oddly enough, no two shared the same fear. Poverty was one man's most pervasive fear. Other fears surfaced—the fear of rejection, the fear of pain, the fear of hell. Even fear of success. The fear of failure is common, but there are people who somehow always manage to snatch failure from the jaws of victory. They behave in ways that insure failure because they are terrified of succeeding.

We learned that day that the personal fears of our small group were just a sample of the kinds of fears most people are plagued with. Fear of the past, fear of the future. Fear of ridicule. Fear of impotence. Fear of old age and the loss of health or beauty; live long enough and you can't avoid that. Fear of being dependent: you may try to lead your life without needing anyone, and in that way, you circumvent hurt and rejection. Again, if you live to extreme old age, you are almost certain to be dependent on family or some impersonal caregiver. Then, there is the fear of making mistakes or the fear of never finding fulfillment. How poignant that last fear is—to live your whole life without ever attaining those things for which you've been striving so hard.

On a human level, there are some common strategies for handling fear. Let's examine some of them.

First of all, we can resign ourselves to living with fear. *Que sera, sera,* as the song says. Whatever will be, will be. This fatalistic philosophy is not at all the same as the doctrine of predestination. Predestination is a belief in an omnipotent, omniscient God who somehow knows our choices, even before we make them. Predestination has nothing to do with fatalism. Fatalists give up: "That's the way life is. There's nothing I can do about it."

Secondly, we can handle our fears by working harder, getting up earlier, putting in longer hours, praying more. We think we can get our lives organized to the place where fear is eliminated. The fallacy here is that we believe we are in control, and that by our efforts we can manipulate almost everything around us: family, friends, even circumstances. Obviously, we can't.

A third way we can react to our fears is by becoming depressed. "What's the use? Things are bad and going to be worse." That's Murphy's Law. To dull the pain, we take pills and alcohol. But by blotting out the pain, we give up our humanity. We no longer suffer, but neither do we love and reach out and contend for the things we care about.

We can also react with anger. That was Cain's response. We feel threatened by something or someone out there. Therefore, rather than changing our own behavior or finding ways to relate, we blame others and go on the attack. This is the scenario being acted out by most abusive parents or abusive spouses, by people who are suicidal or who end up killing others. Basically, they are taking their anger out on themselves or someone else. "Somebody must be to blame for the awful situation I'm in." A case in point is the man in Miami who shot his stockbroker. According to the newspaper accounts, he had made a killing on the market until the crash came and his fortune evaporated. His response was to find a second victim—the broker. The fear of poverty produced uncontrollable anger, which resulted in murder.

Or, we can handle our fear with optimism. Hope for the best, whatever happens. That's a naive way to live life, and I don't recommend it. It may make you easier to live with, but it doesn't change the circumstances of your life. Optimism, with no foundation in fact, is a mild form of mental illness. Of course, I do not speak here of an optimism based on faith in God's power to intervene and to act.

Finally, we can respond to fear by appeasement—peace at all costs. We'll do anything to alleviate our fears. In counseling, this is called co-addiction, adjusting to a loved one's destructive habits as a way of protecting ourselves from our fears. We'll make any accommodation to make life bearable, but those accommodations keep the addict in his or her problem. Absolute peace and security are not attainable goals. Appeasing others to allay our own fears has deadly results.

As we address this whole matter of fear in this and subsequent chapters, let me say at the outset that there is no way to live without fear. Nevertheless, it is possible to live beyond fear. Even those of us who have faith and who trust in God are going to find ourselves in scary situations. We need to learn to appropriate for our lives the reassurance of those words the Lord repeats so often in the Gospels. "Don't be afraid. Fear not."

I learned something new about fear in a talk some years ago with Dr. Paul Tournier, a Swiss physician and author. I asked how he helped his patients get rid of their fears. "I don't," he said. "Fear has a purpose. Everything that has meaning in life is frightening. If you eliminate fear, life closes in." I thought about that later—how each new step in life has its own terrors. We begin by leaving the nest, the safe and comfortable place in which we have been nurtured and protected. We embark on a new career, perhaps move to a new location where we must make new friends. Marriage is often the next step. We commit ourselves to another person for an uncertain future. At each juncture, the next phase looks terrifying. We cannot eliminate the causes of our fear, but we can believe that Jesus is standing at each of those crossroads with us, and we can trust him with the future.

I had a new conversion, about my 893d, some weeks ago. For a month or so, things had seemed to be falling apart in my life, professionally and personally. There were all sorts of administrative problems, committee conflicts; a lot of loose cannons on the deck. My reaction was to get depressed. I came home late one night from a presbytery meeting, even more discouraged. I slept very little that night, awoke at four in the morning, and finally got up at five. I brewed a pot of coffee and began my quiet time. Tucked in my Bible I found a quote of Helen Keller's, that blind, deaf, and mute luminary who accomplished so much in spite of staggering handicaps. She wrote, "Life is a great adventure, or it is nothing. There is no such thing as security. Animals never experience it and children seldom do."

It was a direct word of the Lord for me. My mistake had been in feeling that life should be more secure and free of problems. We envy the animals their worry-free existence, but they have no security. Jesus advised us to "be like the birds," but they have no guaranteed income, no portfolio. They have no lease on the nest. In Jesus' time, two sparrows were sold for a penny and then dropped into the soup pot. Nevertheless, they are carefree, and we are admonished to be like them. "Be like little children," said Jesus. Children

are at the mercy of their parents, good or bad. They have
no real security. They live, happily or unhappily, at the
whim of their elders. I, too, must live like the birds and the
children, with no certainty about the future.

I saw it all clearly. My desire to build a life, a job, a
church, free from problems and anxieties, is the beginning
of constructing a box with four sides and a lid. I can totally
control my environment and, given enough time, I will
decompose in that box six feet underground. Jesus urges me
instead to live the adventure of faith, to make him my
security. Circumstances have not improved dramatically
since that illuminating moment, but I'm having a wonderful
time in the midst of my problems.

I got a letter from one of my fourth-grade friends a
while ago. She had been presented with her first Bible
during morning worship, along with the rest of her Sunday
School class, and she wrote me later to tell how one passage
had helped her. "My favorite book of the Bible is Psalms.
I was staying alone for a while at home, but I heard a bang
and I didn't know what it was. It came from upstairs. I didn't
go upstairs, but I read Psalm 25. It really helped me."

Part of the psalm that spoke to my young friend says,
"Oh guard my life and deliver me; let me not be put to
shame, for I take refuge in Thee" (Ps. 25:20, RSV). She has
discovered how to handle one of her fears—her fear of
strange sounds in the night. In these next chapters we will
be talking about some of our specific fears, and what God,
through both Old and New Testaments, has to say to us
about them.

2. Why Are You Afraid?

Mark's gospel gives us an account of a violent storm at sea. The disciples are terrified, certain they are on the verge of sinking. When they wake Jesus, who has been sleeping on a cushion in the stern, he puts a question to them. "Why are you afraid?" It seems an odd question. Obviously, they have a host of good reasons for being afraid. If I were to write a script of that scene, the dialogue might go like this:

JOHN: Sir, I don't think you have any idea what's been going on while you were sleeping. It was terrifying.

JESUS: Even so, why are you afraid?

MATTHEW: Master, water was coming into the boat. We were certain we would sink.

JESUS: But why are you afraid?

ANDREW: Some of us can't swim, Jesus. If the boat sank, we'd surely drown.

JESUS: And why are you afraid?

PETER: (interrupting excitedly) I think I understand what you're saying. If we have faith in you, nothing bad can happen to us. Isn't that why you're telling us not to be afraid?

JESUS: *(emphatically)* Don't you believe it. Terrible things will happen to *me* in just a short while. They will happen to you as well in the coming years. Bad things can and will happen, in spite of your faith. Nevertheless, why are you afraid?

It's a question he's still asking his disciples. Those of us who have experienced the power of his presence in our lives need not fear, whatever the circumstances. And yet, under duress, we are so quick to feel abandoned and powerless.

Most of us, like the twelve disciples in that storm, have been faced with forces over which we had no control, and we were fearful. We may have actually been in a boat in a storm, one that did sink, or seemed about to. You may have been on a plane that hit an air pocket, or had engine failure, and the end seemed inevitable. I was once on one of those endangered planes. Emergency vehicles were awaiting us at the runway, and we flew out over the ocean to dump our gas. Believe me, we were scared. Or you may have been lost in a mountain wilderness somewhere, separated from your party. That happens with some regularity in my part of the world to skiers and backpackers.

Statistics indicate that a lot of us have been in an out-of-control situation in a car—icy roads, brake failure, or a collision. So many things can cause our ship to flounder on the rocks: divorce, a job loss, economic reverses. We have no way of knowing when we may be faced with cancer or any other dread disease. Being human means that from time to time there will be scary circumstances over which we have little or no control.

Woody Allen, one of our contemporary philosophers, says, "We are at a crossroads. One path leads to despair and utter hopelessness; the other to total extinction. I pray we have the wisdom to choose wisely." Many of us feel like that, both in our personal lives and on a national and international level. Fear, dormant or active, is an emotion we live with almost constantly. Some of us even seek out opportunities to exercise that emotion from time to time at an amusement park, at a scary movie, or with a blood-curdling work of fiction.

I confess that, when I have time for recreational reading, I usually choose a horror story. As a child, I read all the works of Edgar Allen Poe, and now I'm a Stephen King fan. In the introduction to a recent book, he speaks to this fascination of ours for the scary:

Fear makes us blind and we touch each fear with all the avid curiosity of self-interest, trying to make a whole out of a hundred parts, like the blind man with an elephant. We sense the shape. . . . The shape is there and most of us come to realize what it is sooner or later. It is the shape of a body under a sheet. All our fears add up to one great fear. . . . We're afraid of the body under the sheet. It's our body and the great appeal of horror fiction through the ages is that it serves as a rehearsal for our own deaths.

I'd like to think he's right—that all the horror stories I've read over the years make it more possible to face life's genuine horror stories, my own and that of other people.

We talked earlier about the different ways we have of handling fearful situations. Our response is usually instinctual, grounded in our overall response toward life. Let's set up an imaginary scenario. You are driving in a car over a mountain pass in the dead of night. For some reason, you've left the main route and are on a side road. The engine sputters briefly and then stops entirely. You are stuck out in the wilderness, miles from anyone or anything, and you are out of gas.

What would your first reaction be? I think I'd start to berate myself. "Larson, this is a monumentally stupid thing you have done. You've been a jerk before, but this time you've outdone yourself." That might be true, but it's not very creative. You might start rewriting the script. "If I just hadn't started out at night. If only I'd stayed on the main route. Why didn't I watch the gas gauge?" Those "if only" thoughts are unproductive, to say the least, when you're living through a crisis.

Another reaction is to seize on temporary escape: pop a pill, have a few belts from that bottle of Scotch in the trunk, go to sleep until morning comes and, with it, the possibility of help. Some of us would simply be reduced to whining, "Why me? What have I done to deserve this?" Then there's the "blame someone else" response: "I told my son to put gas in this car. It's his fault I'm in this mess." Getting angry and laying blame is another way of dealing with our fears.

The book of Acts gives us the story of the Apostle Paul caught in a fearful situation, a shipwreck. The captain and his crew were sure they would all drown. Paul brought a note of calm and reassurance. He suggested they take time out to eat. "Break out the bread and salami. There's a jug of wine left. Let's have a picnic." Faced with disaster, he was calling for a return to normalcy. His companions were urged to make a commitment to life instead of death.

But let's look again at the account of the storm at sea that so terrified the disciples, and at the events that preceded it. Jesus had been teaching all day long, and if you have ever been a teacher, or in a similar situation, lecturing or answering questions, up to your ears in the press of the crowd, you know how exhausting that is. There was no rest break or time-out for Jesus. I don't think he expected one. Part of the problem with some Christian leaders today is that they believe the demands of the job give them special privileges. They figure they're doing so much for the Lord that they're entitled to a break, in whatever form that takes: custom-tailored suits, luxury cars, even occasional illicit liaisons.

Jesus ministered to the crowd without interruption, but at the end of the day he left them unapologetically. He said to the disciples, "Let us go over to the other side." He was not trapped by his own success. He was able to walk away from this enthusiastic, perhaps even adoring crowd. He left at the peak of a successful meeting to strike out for the unknown. We need to follow his example more in that respect. Once you've started a successful work—especially if it is a mission or ministry which you feel is God's work—you feel trapped forever. You don't see how you can leave and disappoint the many people who count on you. Jesus was free to say good-bye and move on. He had no way of knowing who or what was across the lake, or what kind of reception he would find there.

As events unfold in Mark's Gospel, we find he has left the multitude to help just one person, the Garasene demoniac. God's strategy seldom makes sense from the world's point of view. The mission policies of our churches don't make a lot of sense, economically. We don't approach it by figuring out how many missionaries we can send for the money budgeted. We don't ask, "Where can we get the most for our dollar?" We send missionaries to some high-rent districts, such as Japan and France, when, with that same sum, we could support ten workers in Chad or Bangladesh. But the Christian life is not a matter of cost efficiency. We try to hear God's call and respond. Many are not necessarily better than one. The Kingdom of God has its own economics, and this particular story seems to bear that out.

Mark's Gospel describes their departure in this way: "Leaving the crowd, they took Him with them, just as He was, in the boat" (Mark 5:36, RSV). One of the surprising parts of that sentence is "they took Him along." We might expect it to read, "He took them along." An old and favorite hymn claims, "Where he leads me I will follow." That's a noble sentiment, but it is also true that *he* goes where *you* go. Christ in you, the hope of glory (Col. 1:27). If you go to the right place, he is with you. If you go to the wrong place, he is still with you. Livingston, the great missionary to Africa, was once asked, "How can you walk miles, year after year, all across Africa?" "Because I know I'm not alone," was the reply. "Jesus has said, 'Lo, I am with you always to the end of the age.' I have the word of a gentleman of the strictest honor that he is with me."

On this particular night, Jesus was with the disciples, going wherever they went. But the sentence we are examining continues with another strange twist. "They took Him along, *just as He was.*" I'm not sure what that means. How else could they take him except as he was? Perhaps he was grouchy, tired. Perhaps he was sweaty and dirty from the long, hot day. That phrase, "just as He was," could very well have a wider meaning. We are often tempted to appropriate some imaginary Jesus for our faith walk, some eviscerated Jesus, a Jesus more amenable to our own predisposition and prejudices. We want to make him a liberal or a conservative, a fundamentalist or a charismatic, an evangelical or a liberation theologian. We want a Jesus who espouses our theology and our political beliefs, rather than the historical Jesus of the New Testament.

The storm that came up in the middle of the night was severe enough to strike terror into even the seasoned sailors. Men who had made a livelihood on the sea of Galilee all their adult lives were panicked. They not only woke Jesus, they rebuked him. "Don't you care if we drown?" In other words, "Where are you when we need you?" You have prayed that prayer, and so have I. "Lord, how could you have allowed this to happen to me—or to my mother—or to my son? How can I be in a mess like this? Don't you care?" The rebuke of the disciples has a familiar ring.

Immediately, Jesus rebuked the wind and the waves, and calm returned. The disciples were awed, but those of us on the other side of the resurrection have little difficulty with the story. The God of creation who made the sea and wind can certainly still them. It's at this point in the story, when the danger has passed, that Jesus turns to them with his question, "Why are you afraid? Do you still have no faith?" As we said, our faith doesn't prevent the storms. They come to us all, deserving or undeserving. When and if we are delivered, the tendency is to vow never to get into the boat again. Unfortunately, we cannot live the life of faith in some safe place. Even after we are delivered, we are called to move on to the next adventure where storms are likely to break all over again.

A friend in Canada survived some perilous storms in recent years, storms which would surely have washed away the less courageous. Darryl Potter lives outside Ontario, Canada, and her story was published not long ago under the title, "God's Wonderful Gift to Me." Darryl was born in 1924 in Liverpool, England. Right after World War II, she and her husband emigrated to Canada, where they raised three kids. Both parents worked full time. One day Darryl hit her knee against the filing cabinet in her office and got thrombophlebitis. The next morning, her leg was so swollen she couldn't get out of bed. Subsequently, she endured over a hundred operations. One leg was removed at the hip, the other above the knee. Her right arm was amputated above the elbow and she lost the sight of one eye. It's not surprising that all that surgery led to an addiction to pain pills. In the meantime, her husband was so traumatized by these horrible events that he began to drink and abuse the children. She divorced him. One son went into the navy, but the other two children moved into an apartment with their mom.

It was at this point in her life that Darryl felt she heard the Lord saying to her, "Why are you afraid?" That was a turning point. She presently travels all over Canada and parts of the United States, speaking in schools and hospitals and institutions about helping the handicapped. She writes this:

It is not my missing limbs that matter now, but what is within me that counts. I feel like an oil painting on an easel. So often I will try to jump off that easel to paint myself. . . . If I can stay on that easel, I know He will paint a perfect picture of me, one I could never be ashamed of, a picture so perfect that I will be able to withstand anything, no matter how bad it may be at the time. God's gift to me is life, and it is what I do with this life that will be my gift to Him.

God wants to give us all that gift of life. The storms are going to come, that's certain, and perhaps they already have. We have the option of taking Jesus with us . . . *just as he is.*

II. THE FOCUS OF OUR FEARS

3. The Fear of Making Mistakes

We'd like to think that the Christian life, the guided life, the life committed to God and his purposes, will be a life in which we will make no more mistakes. Unfortunately, the life of faith is a risky adventure, and mistakes are unavoidable. It has been said that If a thing is worth doing, it is worth doing poorly. If you wait to act until you have all you need to assure success, you've probably missed the magic moment. We are to move out into ministry and mission with whatever resources are at hand. We will probably never be totally prepared.

The fear of making a mistake just might be the number one spiritual block for any number of Christians. We suffer from too much caution, and we could theorize forever on how we got that way. Was it overprotective parents, early conditioning, or were we simply born that way? Whatever the reason, too much caution in our lives translates into too little action. Fear of making a mistake paralyzes us, and we miss those God-given opportunities to be a part of his work in the world.

J. B. Fuqua, chairman and founder of one of the largest conglomerates in our land, was quoted in the *Wall Street Journal*. "If you do something you have a fifty-fifty chance of being right. If you do nothing, the world passes you by." I'm told business is looking for managers who can make right decisions just half of the time. They need people who make decisions and move on. A bad decision is better than no decision. The fear of making mistakes blocks success in every area of life. Albert Einstein said, "I think and think for months, for years, and ninety-nine times the conclusion is false. The one hundredth time I am right." Even that remarkable scientist made mistakes before he came up with the revolutionary $e = mc^2$.

A year or so ago, a full-page ad from United Technologies addressed the problem.

Don't be afraid to fail. You've failed many times, only you may not remember. You fell down the first time you tried to walk. You almost drowned the first time you tried to swim, didn't you? Did you hit the ball the first time you swung a bat? Heavy hitters, the ones who hit the most home runs, also strike out a lot. R. P. Macy failed seven times before his store in New York caught on. English novelist John Creasey got 753 rejection slips before he published 564 books. Babe Ruth struck out 1330 times, but he also hit 714 home runs. Don't worry about failure. Worry about the chances you miss when you don't even try.

The fear of making a mistake usually creates a secondary problem, and that is the need to justify ourselves. So much time is wasted explaining precisely why we did make a mistake. In point of fact, nobody cares why. If we could just own it and move on. I think of the many times in my marriage that I've tried to justify my words or actions. "All I said was . . ." "All I did was . . ." The only important thing is that I hurt the person I love most. I hope I'm learning to confess my mistakes more often and move on.

C. S. Lewis, with his peculiar genius, puts his finger on the problem in his book *The Great Divorce.* He paints hell as the place where citizens are free to leave. Heaven, by God's grace, is open to all. But those living in hell prefer to stay there because they cannot admit they were ever wrong. They protest that they were misinformed, or trapped by circumstances. They need only say, "I was wrong" and accept God's unlimited grace to move from Graytown (Lewis' name for hell) to the Celestial City.

At the heart of the universe is costly forgiveness. Luther summed it up with the words, "Love God and sin boldly." There is grace to cover your sins and mine—past, present and future. We are to live in the costly grace God has provided through the death and resurrection of his beloved son. The New Age movement is nowhere more at odds with Christianity than at this point. There are no absolutes except those its adherents set for themselves. The New Age followers purport to be God, and as God, they can make the rules, rewrite the rules, or declare there are no rules. It's like playing tennis without a net. Every ball you hit is a good ball. No judge is needed. New Agers, in declaring everybody God, have removed the mystery and wonder at the heart of the universe, a God of grace who forgives in costly ways.

If we can forgive each other, maybe we can even forgive ourselves. We can be a bit less afraid of making mistakes and spend a little less time in endlessly justifying ourselves.

We have to accept that mistakes are normal—not just personally, but on a national scale as well. Our nation, however much we love it, has not always acted wisely or even honorably over its two-hundred-year history. The war in Vietnam was a monumental mistake from every point of view. It took our young people, marching and demonstrating, to turn the tide and prick the conscience of the nation and stop the long years of pointless slaughter.

Russia, a nation we tend to think of as invincible, was engaged in a stalemate war with Afghanistan for more than eight years. The myth of the invincible Russian army was challenged by a few stubborn mountain people who would not be conquered, a nation on their very borders. Even the Politburo was forced to concede it was a big mistake.

Most of us delight in catching mistakes, especially those in print. UPI, that great news-gathering service, sent out a story on Cardinal Cook's funeral at St. Patrick's Cathedral in New York. Some reporter, obviously not a churchgoer, reported that the closing hymn was, "O God, our Health and Age Has Past." That goof appeared in thousands of papers.

We all agree that a lot of mistakes have been made over the years in the area of education. Things are not getting better and better; far from it. I read that the top seven school discipline problems in the 1940s were, in this order, students talking, chewing gum, making noise, running in the halls, getting out of turn in line, wearing improper clothing, and not putting paper in wastebaskets. In the 1980s, the top problems in our public schools are drug abuse, alcohol abuse, pregnancy, suicide, rape, robbery, assault, burglary, arson, bombings, murder, absenteeism, vandalism; and the list goes on. Our school system is deteriorating, and we are going to have to face the fact that serious mistakes have been made.

It cannot be said often enough that our goal as Christians is not a mistake-free life. The book of Acts is not some whitewashed account of the early church. In it we read about the mistakes of Peter, Paul, and others. Even the choice of a disciple to replace Judas might very well have been a mistake. It does seem that God had Paul in mind all along. God has given us free will. He does not move us about like puppets. If you become a Christian hoping that God will guide your every action, it won't happen. God does from time to time break through with a specific direction—change your job, make an apology, begin a ministry—but much of the time God's will is not at all clear. Our witness is not that we are never wrong, but that God is with us and loves us, right or wrong. He guides us to turn right, and, even though we turn left, he will still be with us going left. We are not infallible, but we belong to a God who is both omnipresent and omniscient. As for me, I'm not sure I'm a better person than I was forty years ago. I may be. I may not. I hope I'm a better person, more mature, more loving, more eager to confess mistakes and move on, but maybe I'm not. It's a moot question.

Maybe our primary witness to the world is in the way we handle our mistakes. That may say more about maturity and perfection than anything else. When we have been caught off base, when something happens that looks like a mistake, we are not surprised by our fallibility. But more than that, we don't try to explain or justify. We simply acknowledge it and try to remedy it.

But there is a possibility that, in terms of crucial life choices, the people who have given their lives to Christ cannot make an irredeemable mistake. Paul wrote to the Romans that "We know that in everything God works for good with those who love Him, who are called according to His purpose" (Rom. 8:28, RSV). It's a testament to the sovereignty of God. In any and all circumstances, he is going to work out his will in the lives of his children.

We will still have moral and ethical dilemmas. We will be tested in all sorts of areas, tomorrow and the next day and in all the succeeding days. Let me give you a strategy for living in those times of testing.

First of all, seek guidance. Pray daily. Sometimes God will give you a clear word, but if he doesn't, remember, he wants a relationship with you. That's more important than guidance.

Secondly, get the facts. If you need to make choices and guidance doesn't come, learn all you can about the situation. God can guide you through your own thought processes and many decisions will be made on the basis of common sense.

Third, wait for the *kairos*. *Kairos* is a Greek word for the moment of opportunity. This may be one of those magic moments when everything falls into place.

Fourth, act boldly. The life of faith is a life of risk. If you are faced with two choices, avoid the safer one.

Fifth, when mistakes happen, relax. Expect God to act. God can make compost out of our failures. He can give us a second chance, as he gave to the prophet Jonah. In the Old Testament story we read that even after Jonah ignored the Lord and did not do what he wanted, the Lord came to Jonah a second time (Jon. 3:1). The Lord can intervene and direct a second time or a third time. He uses all those times to bring about his will.

Sixth, when mistakes occur, admit them. I have been to two different dry cleaners in the years I have been in Seattle. The first promised to have a suit ready for me on a certain day, and when it wasn't, he had a litany of excuses. "We've been busy. It's a holiday. One of our machines broke down. We were shorthanded." I didn't really care about those management problems. My new dry cleaner also disappointed me recently. My suit wasn't ready, but he simply said, "We're terribly sorry. We apologize." He's my man. Something magic happens when a mistake is honestly acknowledged.

A while ago, Continental Airlines took out a full-page ad in magazines and newspapers all across the land to apologize to their customers. The gist of the ads was, "We grew so fast we made mistakes, misplaced baggage. There were delays, reservation errors. You were frustrated and angry, and a lot of hardworking people at Continental were pretty embarrassed." I hope their strategy mollified their unhappy travelers and gained some new ones. An honest apology is worth a hundred excuses.

Of course, an apology alone is not sufficient. There must be a serious effort to remedy our mistakes. I read an article this past year about Coleman stoves. They were having a problem with the burners. The service department met to discuss the problem. Armed with clipboards and yellow pencils, everybody hunkered down for a serious discussion on how to manage this mess. Financial and legal obligations would be assessed and customer relations analyzed. But old man Coleman, the founder of the company, nipped all those strategies in the bud. "You mean," he said, "we have goods out there that don't work? Get them back and find out why. Replace them." That was the end of the meeting.

Not a bad model for you and me. Let's admit our mistakes and fix things if we possibly can. I would urge you to make more mistakes. It would mean you are living the life of faith with more abandon, and God can use even our mistakes. They may even prove to be a part of his larger plan.

4. The Fear of Success

Earlier we touched on the fact that the fear of success can be documented just as much as the fear of failure. There is a fish story in Luke's Gospel, the success of which outdoes any other fish story we've heard before or since. But, oddly enough, Simon Peter's reaction to that record catch was fear. Let's examine the details.

This remarkable fish story occurs in Galilee, a very provincial part of the empire and the place where Jesus began his ministry. The events leading to this particular fishing tale are fast-moving and attention-getting. First, Jesus reads scripture and speaks in the synagogue, where his hearers are both confounded and offended. Next, an evil spirit is driven out of a deranged man. In the home of Simon Peter, Jesus restores the big fisherman's mother-in-law to health. This attracts a whole flock of people with physical ailments, all of whom are healed.

In the wake of all these hectic activities, we find Jesus teaching and preaching at the edge of the Sea of Galilee. Two boats have just come in, and the fishermen are washing their nets. The sight gives Jesus an idea for crowd control. He steps into Simon Peter's boat and, pushing out from land, continues to teach and preach. In a similar situation today, the preacher would probably send out for portable amplifiers or some kind of raised platform. Jesus demonstrates for us here and in many other situations that we are to make use of whatever is at hand, those resources already in place and which will work quickly and expeditiously.

Simon Peter's boat becomes the platform from which Jesus can teach and preach.

Some years ago when I worked in Manhattan, I was in a men's lunch group with a man who was deeply concerned about finding ways to minister to Christians working in those concrete canyons. Convinced that they needed a quiet place to go and pray in the midst of the hustle and bustle, he was trying to raise money to rent space for a midtown chapel. It seemed like a great idea. At a later lunch meeting, however, a commercial artist in the group came up with a better solution. "I'm not at all sure we need that," said Bob. "It seems to me God has already provided us with thousands of prayer chapels all over Manhattan, courtesy of the telephone company. You can step into any phone booth in the city, close the door behind you, take the phone off the hook, and pray." That was the end of our friend's effort to raise money for a chapel.

Jesus preempted Peter's boat for his pulpit, but afterward he had a plan to reward him. He suggested that they put out to sea and let down their nets for a catch. Peter was skeptical. He explained that they had already fished all night with no luck. Anybody in the fishing business knows that's the time to catch fish, not in broad daylight with the sun glaring on the water and spooking the fish. He did as Jesus asked, but we can imagine what was going through his mind. "Lord, you may be able to cast out demons and heal the sick and preach with authority. You know about spiritual things, but *I* know about fishing. Fishing is my life."

We can understand Peter's reaction. Imagine, if you will, that the most godly person you have ever met—be it a pastor, teacher, friend, or family member—began to tell you how to do your job better. For the sake of conjecture, let's suppose that Mother Teresa, that godly, faith-filled saint who has helped people to live and die with grace all over the world, came to your home town on a speaking tour. You managed to meet her and to invite her to visit you at your place of business. Let's say you are a very successful real-estate agent. In our imaginary scene Mother Teresa says, "I see from your financial records you only did five million dollars' worth of business last year. You're missing some obvious possibilities. Let me show you some things you can do to earn fifty million dollars next year." We'd like to think we would react well in that situation, but I have a hunch we might be just as likely to say, "Listen, Mother, stick to helping the poor. Real estate is my business."

Fortunately, Peter, expecting only failure, obeys Jesus. They head out, put down the nets and reap the biggest catch in Peter's career. The weight of it is breaking the nets, and they have to draft their partners in the second boat to join them and help with the haul.

This fishing trip, perhaps the most famous such trip in all history, happens in the aftermath of one of Jesus' preaching missions, and, for me, that raises some interesting possibilities. It suggests that there is no division between the sacred and the secular in the mind of God. We may accept Jesus as the one who forgives our sins and saves our souls and reconciles us to God, but is it possible that he knows the intricacies of your job better than you do?

An old friend from my first parish made that very discovery. He was an executive officer of a firm building amplifiers, one of the best known in the world. Sid was a new Christian and beginning to try to take his faith to work with him each day. Here is the story he told. The firm had just introduced a whole new line of amplifiers and, to their dismay, none of them worked. Ph.D.s in the labs tested all of the parts and couldn't figure out the problem. If all those machines had to scrapped, the year's profits would be lost.

"I decided to pray about it," said Sid. "I went to my office, closed the door, got on my knees and asked Jesus for help. Even as I prayed, the crazy idea came to me that two wires were somehow crossed. It didn't seem to make sense, but I tried it and, believe it or not, that did the trick. We got all the sets working. It seems Jesus knows more about electronics than our whole staff of Ph.D.s."

An old friend is an Episcopal layman and physician, a man of God who has been a Christian for a long time. He shared his account of an emergency operation that seems equally curious. He was operating on a twelve-year-old boy who had been gored by a bull. His insides were full of manure and straw and mud, and as they tried to clean him out and sew up all the ruptures, my friend came to a stuck point. There seemed no way to save this twelve-year-old lad. "I began to pray," said my friend. "In the calm that came to ease my panic, a possible procedure occurred to me, though I had never heard of it before. As a result, that boy lived, praise God. Later, I tried to find that procedure in my medical books and I couldn't. I can only believe that picture of how to save the boy's life came directly from God."

Andrew Carnegie, the multimillionaire industrialist and financier, said, "The secret behind my success is that I listen to the nudges that I think I get in the wee, small hours of the night."

When we put our lives under the lordship of Jesus, we are prone to think that there are compartments of that life that we don't need any help with. Getting specific guidance or nudges in our area of expertise can make us less than comfortable. In the fishing excursion we have discussed, Peter is terrified by his instant success. Jesus speaks to him, as he does to us: "Don't be afraid." And he goes on to call him and his companions to a more important work, work more exciting than catching a ton of fish. They are, in the future, to catch men—to capture the hearts and minds of people for the Kingdom of God

We are amazed to read that after getting all those fish ashore, Simon and his companions "left everything and followed Him" (Luke 5:11, RSV). They didn't even stay long enough to clean the fish and market them. The biggest catch of their lives was insignificant in the light of the new call to be a part of that special band for the next three years.

Peter's unexpected success made him fearful, and that's the very point we want to address here. There are people who are chronically fearful of success, and I'm sure those patterns start early on. Counselors, psychiatrists, physicians, tell us that there are those people who are determined never to succeed in life. We're told that compulsive gamblers are like that. They can't quit while they're ahead. They're programmed to stay in the game until they lose. One explanation is that it is a kind of justification for all of the other areas of failure in one's life. "What do you expect of me? I can't seem to win at anything."

That fear-of-success syndrome can affect pastors. They move from one unhappy situation to another and can only accept a call to a church where failure is inevitable, or so it seems. I'm sure you've known people in business or the professions with that problem. It starts early on, psychologists tell us.

One test they give children involves tossing rope rings around a peg set in a wooden block. The instructions are deliberately sketchy. The children are given the rings and told that the point of the game is to get them over the peg. Some children set the peg down right in front of them, drop the ring over the peg and win every time. They are terrified of failure and play in a way that assures success. That behavior takes all the fun out of the game, but they can't lose. Another group puts the peg at a reasonable distance and sometimes they win and sometimes they lose. But they understand that is the challenge of the game. Then there are the children who put the pegs so far away that they can't possibly reach them. There is no chance of success. That behavior, unfortunately, follows them through life. They choose unsatisfying mates and unrewarding jobs which seem to insure failure.

In too many cases, failure is a choice, however unconscious, and so is much of our unhappiness. I would bet that you who have had houseguests have followed this script. I know we have:

"What do you want for breakfast?"

"Anything. Whatever you're having."

"Actually, we have everything. Eggs, bacon, cereal, even oatmeal. What would you like?"

"It doesn't matter. Whatever you're going to have is fine."

You end up totally frustrated in your desire to come up with something pleasing and, of course, this script is repeated with all the decisions of the visit—choosing restaurants, movies, places of interest. We have to conclude that there are people who are determined never to be joyful. There are those couples who have been married for more years than they can count who fight all the time. That's what keeps them together—their shared misery is the fuel of the relationship.

The "Peanuts" cartoon is written by one of my favorite theologians, Charles Schultz, and he often zeroes in on this syndrome. One cartoon has Lucy saying to Charlie Brown, "You know, life is like an ocean liner. Some people take their deck chair and put it on the stern, to see where they have been, and some put their deck chair on the bow, to see where they are going. Charlie Brown, tell me, where do you want to put your deck chair?" He says, "I can't even unfold my deck chair." Charlie Brown, the eternal loser, has a fear of success.

Even our choice of a church, or a church leader, is an indication of our feelings about success. For the sake of example, let's think about two extremes—Jimmy Swaggart and Robert Schuller. Swaggart preaches a hell-fire-and-brimstone-you'd-better-shape-up gospel. His hearers eat it up. It's like being beaten with a velvet whip. It doesn't do any permanent damage, and it feels so good. Schuller's congregation is being told that they can make it. God loves them and wants to bless them. We have to face the fact that that is not a universally appealing message. There are a lot of people out there who enjoy getting whipped once in a while, and they especially enjoy hearing how bad the rest of the world is.

Soon after I arrived in my present parish, a couple took me aside to register a complaint. "Since you've been here, we seem to laugh a lot in worship. We don't think that's appropriate." I had to level with them. "You may be right, but while I'm here, we're going to laugh. I think laughter has a legitimate place in worship." Laughter is one of the hallmarks of emotional success, and there are people who avoid even that.

There are segments of the Christian church afflicted with this fear-of-success syndrome. They represent the antithesis of the health-and-wealth gospel. As for the latter, their faith in a God who is supposed to make them rich and keep them well seems patently self-serving. But at the opposite end of the spectrum are those who prefer a church where the carpets are threadbare, the roof leaks, and the pastor is grossly underpaid. Even a dwindling membership is a virtue. It is a sign that the "true" gospel is being preached, rather than a "popular" one.

Hear me. There is no intrinsic virtue in being either poor or joyless. Jesus said that he came that we might have joy and have it abundantly. A friend from New England wrote, "Frugality is not one of God's virtues. He does not save small pieces of string. God's economy is wildly extravagant. God tosses into space a million stars and suns and planets, whirling and dancing in their galaxies, yet only one is a carrier of breathing, singing life." It is mind-boggling to contemplate that God may have caused a billion galaxies to produce one earth and begin a strange experiment with people made in his image.

If God wants to bless us, then let the blessings come. If God wants to overwhelm us with success, even an immense catch of fish, let's just say thank you. We need not fear success at any level—emotional, financial, relational, or spiritual. But keep in mind that our personal success or failure is secondary to the success or failure of the battle being waged between principalities and powers. That is the battle for which Jesus recruited Peter and his companions. The word for *catch* in the original Greek is *zogreo,* which means *to take alive.* We are to go out and, in the term used by the famous big game hunter Frank Buck, "Bring them back alive."

There are at least two major lessons to be learned from the story of the big catch. First, in the mind of God, there is no separation between secular or sacred. Second, God is on our side, and he wants us to succeed. Plan for success. Don't fear it. We have an extravagant God who wants to bless us at the right time and in the right way—with a load of fish or whatever else is appropriate to our time and circumstances.

5. The Fear of the Supernatural

The Christian faith is based on events so bizarre that, as someone has said, you couldn't make them up. They are, for the most part, accounts of the supernatural, and that is frightening to all of us. Let's start with the Christmas story, the events surrounding Jesus' birth. They are so unexplainable that they are an offense to the unbeliever.

For the past two thousand years we have been celebrating that event and observing that birthday, and the celebration has produced all sorts of traditions. Some seem almost magical. The Scrooges begin to care for the Tiny Tims. The comfortable care for the afflicted in tangible and personal ways. But there is another side to the Christmas tradition.

For most of us, the season is a time of comfortable routine. We manage Christmas. We give the same presents to the same people with few variations. We send cards to the same list of people, and the cards themselves are undistinguishable from one year to the next. The same holiday parties are attended or given with similar menus. The tree is decorated with the same ornaments each year. Each one is familiar and meaningful. We play the same glorious music on the record player. We go to church knowing what to expect from the sermons, the pageants, the carols and liturgy. In a world full of uncertainty, where stock markets can crash or famines break out, where injustice and abuse are rampant, Christmas is a welcome return to the familiar and, best of all, I can manage it.

The first Christmas, by contrast, is fraught with the supernatural. The old priest, Zechariah totters into the temple to offer his prayers, and he sees the Angel Gabriel. He is told that he and his aging wife will have their first baby, but he flatly disbelieves the angel and, consequently, is struck mute. He does not speak a word until the baby is born. Elizabeth, past youth, barren, and disappointed, finds herself pregnant, and in time gives birth to John the Baptist.

Mary, her teenage cousin, has never had sexual intercourse, and yet this same angel, Gabriel, tells her she will bear a son, if she is willing. And her child is to be the Messiah. She was surely one of the bravest people of all time, this young woman whose life was interrupted by the supernatural. Then there's Joseph, her fiancé. He has a hard time believing Mary's story. Wouldn't you? An angel appears in his sleep to reassure him and to let him know it's all part of God's plan. Joseph believes the unbelievable and marries his fiancé. I'm sure his friends are thinking he has been duped, but Joseph's life is now out of his control and in God's hands.

At the time of the baby's birth, another unusual event takes place—the census. Every male of the Roman Empire is ordered back to his birthplace to register. The whole world, including Joseph and Mary, is uprooted and on the move. But that also means the baby will be born in the place the prophets predicted, Bethlehem. The actual birth is an emergency event. The Messiah is born in a dirty, windy, unkempt stable with no baby clothes, no safety pins, no diapers. From the world's point of view, that is a far cry from the careful planning which surrounds childbirth today, at least in the western world.

Christianity is deeply rooted in the supernatural. That idea is still an affront to a good many people, even some within the Christian camp. In the liberal group there are those who would reduce our faith to good works. Christianity is the vehicle for caring for the poor, fighting for justice, helping the weak and the sick. In part it is that, but we dare not cut out the heart of our faith, the supernatural, God in Christ, reconciling the world to himself. Even the fundamentalists ignore the supernatural, except as a part of our holy history. In its place, they have fundamentalist theology. Any present-day sign of the supernatural power of the Holy Spirit is suspect.

On the secular scene, we have the philosophies of the sixties and early seventies. The young and even middle-aged dropped out, smoked a little grass, wove baskets, and threw rocks at the establishment. At the center of the movement was a form of nihilism. Nothing mattered, neither the rational nor the supernatural. We do only what feels good. The followers of the New Age movement of the eighties emphasize the supernatural, but they create their own out-of-body experiences with the right crystals or a channeler.

Religion, per se, has embraced and produced a lot of strange beliefs and practices over the years. I talked to a man last year who had lost a member of his family. He was angry with God, and, as his pastor, I caught some of that anger. Later he tried to apologize somewhat. "I'm sorry I was so rough on you, preacher, but I'm not big on religion." "Neither am I," I replied. He was flabbergasted. "Religion," I explained, "is a means of manipulating God to get him to do what we want by the proper forms or practices. We Christians believe in a supernatural God who has called us to be his people. He takes the initiative. We are the obedient children."

As we said, the supernatural is at the center of the Christian gospel, and that is fearsome. It is for the shepherds who hear that angelic choir on a dark night on the hills near Bethlehem. Their reaction is understandable. These pathetic, impoverished minimum-wage earners were not prepared for an encounter with angels. We can see it from their perspective, as we put the events in present-day terms. Let's say you have come home from a Christmas Eve service and have tucked yourself and your family into bed. At two-thirty in the morning, you get up to make your way to the bathroom. Walking down the hall, you are hailed by an angel who calls you by name. You might respond with joyful surprise. "Wow! I always knew you guys were there, but I never expected to see you." But I think most of us would be more wary. "Wait a minute. I like angels in pageants at church. I'm not ready for a real one." With glory everywhere, most of us would be scared witless. The shepherds are, of course, Jews, God's chosen people. They belong to that devout band who knows God and expects deliverance at his hand. For centuries the Jews have longed for, prayed for the Messiah. But we can theorize on how some particular groups of people might have reacted on that awesome night, and why.

Had that angelic choir on that wondrous night appeared to a group of scientists, they might have had a legitimate reason for being afraid. Scientists assume that even if God was the creator of the world, he has wound it up, turned it on, and departed. Scientific truth is clearly defined. If you can't measure it, weigh it, taste it, touch it, feel it, see it, it's not real. If I've spent my whole life being a chemist, physicist, or mathematician, I would not adjust to the supernatural with any degree of ease. We could predict that, had a group of scientists been watching the sheep on that memorable night, they would have been utterly terrified.

The choir with its momentous news might have been received with cynicism by a second group; the legalists, those who believe that if God should break through with a message, it would be one of judgment. "Repent. Doom is at hand." Those are the same people who insist that God sent the AIDS epidemic. They believe that God sends famine and all other disasters. You would expect no good results from meeting an angel if you were one of those people.

But even faithful, honest, hardworking people like the shepherds might interpret the strange happenings that night as an unwelcome interruption. They are not part of the usual agenda. "Wouldn't you know it? The supernatural crashed into my life on this dark night, and there go all my plans. I was hoping to go out with the boys and party a little when I finished this shift. God has broken into my life, and I have to scrap all that. I have to embark on a strange journey and witness some mysterious events. I am no longer in control of my life." If that was, in some measure, the basis for the fear of the shepherds, we can identify.

At the heart of sin is our own self-centeredness. I want to be at the center, and I want family members to move around this nice, model person and do exactly what I want. I'll never yell or pout. I'll be reasonable and kind, as long as you all do what I want. At a subconscious level, I expect even God to do my bidding.

In the case of the shepherds, this dramatic interruption necessitates resorting all their priorities, and that is a fearful prospect.

An encounter with the supernatural, then and now, is frightening and, at the very least, inconvenient. His Holy Spirit at work in our lives cannot always be explained reasonably and rationally. God is still sending his messengers to guide us. Sometimes they look very much like our own friends and family members.

A Christian friend with whom I meet weekly is planning to embark on a new career. He feels that God has directed him in midlife to drop out of his present field and enter law school. Of course, a good many people drop out of successful careers and become students again in order to try something new. It's hard to document my friend's experience as a supernatural interruption. But I know at least one story that can only be described that way.

Our oldest son, Peter, a journalist for over ten years, was driving one afternoon from Dallas to Tyler, Texas. He picked up a hitchhiker, which has been his habit over the years. He learned that his passenger had been newly released from prison. As they were driving along, the man asked Peter if he believed in Jesus. That started a two-hour conversation in which the two discussed their personal experiences of God's power. According to Peter, his Jeep seemed full of fire. Eventually, the man got out, never to be seen again. But Peter will never be the same. "God got my attention," he says. He has just graduated from Princeton Theological Seminary and is now in the pastorate.

A young woman in our congregation had been thinking off and on about some kind of mission work. She was riveted by a recent notice in our Sunday bulletin. It was brief: "Needed in Mozambique, a single woman, CPA, with a specialty in financial matters. Must speak Portuguese." You might say there wouldn't be a lot of those people around. The ad was an exact description of Barbara. She promptly sold her CPA practice and her condo and has headed out for the World Mission Office in Mozambique, which, incidentally, is the most needy country in Africa just now.

Fear of the supernatural is understandable. Such experiences will play havoc with our carefully controlled lives. Welcome those interruptions, even though they look frightening. God will provide the resources to handle them. Remember that giant of a man, Goliath, who challenged the members of the Jewish army to a contest? They were all certain he couldn't be beaten. He was too big. David, the young shepherd boy, saw it differently. "He's so big, I can't miss him." Of course, he killed the giant, armed only with a slingshot.

In the Old Testament, Isaiah gives us a prediction of the Messiah's coming and the changes which that event would eventually bring. Lions and lambs will lie down together. Children will play on the holes of snakes and scorpions and asps. Lions will eat straw. Ridiculous supernatural stuff, you may say. I understand your scepticism. It has not happened yet. But it is consistent with the supernatural events described in both Old and New Testaments, none more seemingly preposterous than those which surround that first Christmas.

6. The Fear of Missing Out

Let's turn our attention in these next pages to a fear that underlies a lot of our other fears and about which little has been spoken or written. It is the fear of missing out, of falling short of all the goals and dreams we had for our lives.

At a championship football game between the Denver Broncos and the Cleveland Browns, there was a fumble on the three-yard line in the last minute or so of play. The Cleveland Browns went down to defeat as a result of that goof. Doesn't that represent everyone's nightmare? In the game of life, our team will be counting on us and we will fail. In this case, months of work and exercise and training by hundreds of people were blown away by the last-minute fumble of one man on the three-yard line.

Speaking of nightmares, my wife and I each have recurring ones. Hers involves our three children, now all grown and producing children of their own, but she still has dreams that she has a baby somewhere that she has forgotten all about and has left lying out in the rain or abandoned somewhere. As for me, I have what you'd call a vocational nightmare. I am standing in the pulpit at St. Patrick's, a Roman Catholic cathedral in New York. It is packed to overflowing, and I can't think of a thing to say, and I am without a single note. In the dark watches of the night, there is the disquieting thought that we have, in some invisible court, been weighed and found wanting, that we have fallen short of all we wanted to be and do in life.

If there is in each of us some such ever-present fear, we must assume that we also have, however unformed, some goal we are working toward, some direction we want our life to take. We all have dreams, secret or confessed, modest or grandiose, and those dreams vary from person to person. Some are unashamedly aiming for wealth or fame or power; others dream of unlimited sex, and still others of romance, and those are not necessarily the same thing. If you doubt that, remember that millions of people are hooked on romance novels, which are mostly just titillating, rather than explicitly sexual. You may dream of wisdom or beauty, of physical prowess or spirituality. You may be aiming at artistic creativity or charismatic leadership in some area such as sports or business or government.

You may even dream of becoming a missionary—especially as you read stories about Livingstone or Schweitzer or our present-day Mother Teresa. A seminary student once confessed that his ambition in life was to be a returned missionary. He had no desire to go and serve in a backward country among primitive people, but he thought it would be wonderful to go from church to church afterward, showing slides and sharing his colorful experiences.

When I was twenty-four years old, I had two great dreams. First, I wanted to serve God. He had invaded my heart and my life, and I wanted to be his person, whatever that meant. But just as pressing was the desire to marry. I was so lonely, so eager to share my life with some wonderful woman who would also, of course, be attractive, sexy, and spiritual. I had about given up hope when I met my wife. We were married nine months later, but even during that short time I was certain that this longed-for event would never happen. She would die, or I would, or she might even change her mind. I spent those nine months in fear that I would miss out on this great gift.

As we move through life, our dreams change, as they probably should. Often it's a result of some life-changing encounter. Malcolm Muggeridge, one of Britain's most brilliant writers and thinkers, put his considerable gifts to work to serve God after he met Mother Teresa some years ago. Psychiatrist Gerald S. Jampalsky also credits Mother Teresa with a turning point in his life. They met in Los Angeles. His story is that he had been looking all his life for peace with God, the kind of peace this little Yugoslavian nun radiated. She was on her way to Mexico. He asked if he might accompany her, explaining that he wanted to learn about inner peace from her. Her response was something like this: "Dr. Jampalsky, if you want inner peace, I suggest you donate the price of a round-trip ticket to Mexico City to the poor and stay home." Mother Teresa refused to be his guru. Inner peace comes from God.

Most of us have to settle for not having our dreams fulfilled. We never make the first team. We come to terms with the fact that we may not marry, or be successful, or get rich. We make peace with reality. We won't be a football great, a movie star, or a spiritual giant somewhere between St. Francis and Billy Graham.

Even those who make the first team can miss out later on. In high school I wanted so much to have a leading part in the high school play. I got it and blew my lines. You can marry the person you want most in the world and jeopardize that with some senseless affair. You blow it all in some unthinking, ungodly moment. Bunky Hunt and his brothers seemed to have it all. Together they managed to corner the silver market. Unfortunately, today's victories are likely to be tomorrow's defeats. He is presently close to bankruptcy. His fellow Texan, John Connelley, once one of the wealthiest men in the state, was forced to sell all he owned at public auction.

A man in Denver took out an ad in the *Rocky Mountain News* with this message: "Will trade my non-cooking and non-shopping wife with attitude problem for one Super-bowl ticket. Call Jim. Hurry." A phone number was listed. The media picked up on this item and tracked him down in Chicago, where he had gone to attend a wedding. I think he was smart to leave Denver. At any rate, he told reporters he would gladly trade his wife of eighteen years for one week of happiness. When told about the ad, his wife Sharon pronounced, "He's dead meat." Channel 7 in Denver hooked them up via satellite to discuss the matter. His first words, naive to say the least, were, "Honey, am I in trouble?" We have to wonder how he got to that point. I am sure he once wanted that woman more than anything else in the world, and now he would trade her for a Superbowl ticket.

Life is sometimes like that. You get exactly what you want and end up with ashes. Alexander the Great is said to have cried because there were no new worlds to conquer. Conquering the known world was not enough. The most adored sex goddess in the world, consort to presidents, married to a famous baseball star and a successful playwright, took her own life. Then there are the TV evangelists who reach millions weekly or even daily with the gospel. For some it wasn't enough. It was all jeopardized for a one-night stand in Florida or a rendezvous with a hooker. One even made a run for the presidency. His present level of success was not rewarding enough.

A recent cartoon depicted a businessman in a three-piece suit lying on a psychiatrist's couch, in the middle of a crying, pounding tantrum. "I want to take over Zip Co Industries and they won't let me," is the caption. As if one more big deal would finally translate into happiness. Blaise Pascal, seventeenth-century mystic and scientist, suggested that if we are separated from God we have only two choices.

We make ourselves gods or we end up living to satisfy our senses.

There is a scene from a long-ago movie called *Lovers and Other Strangers* that has stayed with me over the years. A father and son are discussing the son's impending divorce at the kitchen table. The father, an earthy, blue-collar type, says, "So what's the story, Richie? Why?" The son tries to explain. "Because we feel there must be something more." "We all feel there must be something more," is the father's response." "Well, then," asks the son, "why don't you leave Mom and go out and get it, Dad?" The father answers, "Because there is nothing more." It's a cynical statement, but from a secular point of view, it is perfectly true. The next thing won't do it, or even the next after that.

How then can we be sure that we will not miss out? Jesus outlines the way clearly. "Seek first the Kingdom." The other things will come, those things that make for lasting joy. If we are seeking the Kingdom second, or in addition to our personal ambitions, we are destined for disappointment.

There is some good news in this materialistic society of ours. *Newsweek* and some other magazines are declaring that the age of the yuppies is over. Their very success is responsible for their demise. The yuppies finally got their Porsches and BMWs and hot tubs and CD players and VCRs and exotic vacations, and they are left with undefined longings for something more. The age of the yuppies is probably not over for those who haven't made it, but those who have are looking for something else. Augustine's well-known words still apply. "My heart is restless until it rests in thee."

From boyhood on, I wanted to be a lawyer. My later conversion and call to the ministry interrupted all that. But

I always had the feeling that God owed me one, that I had missed out on a great career. I could have been a rich, successful, maybe even famous lawyer. I now have two lawyers in the family—a son and a daughter, and I'm beginning to understand what the law requires. I could not have mastered it in a million years. I would have been a financial and professional failure. God saved me from that disaster. I'm not saying that law is more or less important or rewarding than preaching. I know of a good many unhappy preachers. As we seek first the Kingdom, we will find a job commensurate with our own gifts and needs. God who made us knows how to make use of our particular resources when we let him guide us.

I was discussing all this with my son Peter, who is a recent seminary graduate. He said, "Dad, I've heard people compare God to a wise and kindly coach who knows who should play and when, and in what position. But life is not some game. God owns the whole franchise. He owns both teams. He owns the stands and the hot dog sellers and the parking lot. We are serving the franchise owner of all creation, and if you realize that, it doesn't matter whether or not you are always in the game. He may take you out of the game and send you to the locker room to minister to the man who gives out towels and who just lost a child. God will take care of the game. They'll play without you. Go where he sends you and where he needs you to minister. If you work for the franchise owner, where you happen to be serving is not all that important."

Remember, a good many biblical heroes died before they achieved their goals. Moses is a good example. He died on the edge of the Promised Land. Our only goal is to have the Lord of life say, "Well done, good and faithful servant." That's all we need. We don't need Mom to bless us, or our spouse, or our kids. We don't need the blessings of our boss or of the pope.

A high school classmate of mine died this year of cancer of the esophagus. He was the object of many prayers for healing in his church before he entered Johns Hopkins for surgery. I called him before he left. "Bruce," he told me, "I can't miss. I've had prayers by God's people for healing, and I believe God can heal. If he does, I've got it made. If I die, I've got it made. Either way, I want to serve the Lord and his Kingdom." My friend Bill had no fear of missing out. He was focused on God and his Kingdom, sick or well, in this world or the next.

I envy his unwavering trust on those dark days when those fears arise in me and it's hard to believe the franchise owner knows what he's about. That's when Jesus' words are most meaningful. Seek ye first the Kingdom, and all else—all else—will be added to you.

7. The Fear of Death

I have had a number of close calls with death over the years. Six of those incidents are still vivid. When I was a toddler, I was riding in a car with my parents when the rear door opened suddenly and flung me out onto the highway. A number of cars actually drove over me, but fortunately none of them hit me, and I was not seriously injured. During World War II, there were three separate occasions when my survival seemed miraculous. One winter night, a piece of shrapnel hit the foxhole I was sharing with another man, blowing him to bits and leaving me unharmed. A little later on, I was standing at a window in Heilbronn, directing mortar fire with a fellow sergeant, when a sniper's bullet picked him off with deadly aim. Again, in that same town, an amphibious tank was shot out from under me as we tried to cross the Neckar River. I was the last man to crawl out the hatch before the vehicle sank to the bottom.

In more recent years, I was a passenger on an airplane with faulty landing gear, approaching Kennedy Airport. Fire trucks and ambulances were waiting on the runway. We made it. About ten years ago, I very nearly drowned in the Gulf of Mexico and spent hours in storm-tossed seas before a timely rescue by a tugboat.

I don't know how many such near-death experiences you have had, but the point is that there are for all of us many more we don't know about. Death blew on our cheek or nudged our shoulder, and we weren't even aware that we had come close to dying. In life, we are always a heartbeat away from death. One day, of course, it won't be a close call. It will be our turn.

People of all places and ages have been fascinated by death. I did not realize until recently how general mummification was in ancient Egypt. It was not a process reserved only for kings and pharoahs. Anyone who could afford it was mummified. We Americans put the bulk of our income into instruments of death, arms, nuclear and otherwise, while the Egyptians put theirs into embalming the dead. Followers of the New Age movement tell us that we are all recyclable, like aluminum cans. Their emphasis on reincarnation is another attempt to comprehend and explain the mystery of death.

In recent years, there has been a rash of books out about people who have returned from death, and who report on the experience. By that I mean they were clinically dead, verifiably, and returned to life. I've even seen a video about a man who claimed that happened to him. These accounts are strangely similar and, almost without exception, overwhelmingly positive. For the most part, here's how they read: "I found myself at the death scene, watching people work to revive me. I knew I was dying, pain disappeared, and I slipped into darkness. I entered a long, dark tunnel, almost like a birth canal, with a pinhole of light at the end. I emerged into a beautiful landscape with trees, rivers and waterfalls. I saw family and friends who had died earlier." The final stage is invariably a confrontation with a huge pillar of light which seems to radiate love, joy, and peace. That last experience is the one remembered most vividly in later years. Authentic or not, we find these stories reassuring.

Norman Vincent Peale tells about a vision his stepmother had, shortly after the death of his father. She saw him standing in her darkened bedroom and she seemed to hear him say, "Don't worry about dying. There's nothing to it." That was a source of comfort to this new widow, and to her two sons. But, however positive the reports on life after death, nobody who is physically and emotionally healthy is eager to die. Peale himself is now past ninety, and he claims he plans to live to be a hundred. He is not in a hurry to move on.

In the Netherlands, euthanasia is practiced widely. It is not legal, but it is countenanced under strict conditions. It is believed that from one thousand to seven thousand people a year are put to sleep by their physicians, with the consent of the family and, if possible, the patient. The proponents of this practice believe that we have the freedom to live by our own convictions, and that includes the freedom to die by our own convictions.

As far as I'm concerned, life is a gift of God, and I have no right to destroy that gift in my own case, or in anyone else's. A living will, on the other hand, gives us the chance to exercise our options. We ought not to be forced to prolong life by extreme measures, long after it has any purpose or meaning. It is understandable that the very old and the very infirm have no desire to continue. My mother, in her nineties, often expressed her willingness to die with the phrase, "I want to go home."

But the younger people in our society who are choosing to die in alarming numbers have missed what life is all about. Ralph Burton, the nationally known cartoonist, took his life, leaving this note: "I have done this because I am tired of inventing devices for getting through twenty-four hours every day."

But even those of us who consider ourselves Jesus people can suffer from boredom and depression. Those are times for reevaluating our patterns and priorities. The life Christ offered repeatedly to his disciples was one of adventure and joy.

Nevertheless, no healthy person, vigorous and emotionally sound, chooses death. However and whenever it comes, peaceful or violent, timely or otherwise, it is the last great enemy. Again the reassuring words come from Jesus. "I am the resurrection and the life. He that believeth in me, though he die, yet shall he live" (John 11:25, RSV). Jesus, the Lord of life and of death, has overcome that final enemy.

Abraham Lincoln was criticized generally for his generosity to our nation's enemies in the South in the wake of the Civil War. At a social gathering, one woman saw fit to take him to task. "Mr. President, your responsibility is not to be kind to your enemies, but to destroy them." He was overheard to reply, "But, madam, do I not destroy my enemies when I make them my friends?" It is a sound strategy, and the one used in the peace terms after World War II. Our bitter enemies, Japan and Germany, have since become our strongest allies. In like manner, Jesus has made death, that old enemy, a friend. If you bet your life on that, you can move on to old age and beyond unafraid.

When C. S. Lewis lost his mentor and friend, Charles Williams, who had been instrumental in his conversion, he said, "Heaven is no longer a strange place for me, or a far-off place. I have a friend there." The death of the beloved wife he had married late in life brought heaven even closer for Lewis.

A look at the story of the raising of Lazarus in the 11th Chapter of John's gospel may give us some help in this matter of facing death. His sisters, Mary and Martha, were suffering the loss of a loved one, which can happen to any of us at any time. Certainly, all of us will die, as Lazarus did.

Jesus had been appraised of the situation earlier. "Lord, he whom you love is ill" (John 11:3, RSV). That seems to put to rest the nonsense that if you have enough faith you'll never get sick. Sickness and death come to all, even those whom the Lord loves.

A subsequent verse in this same account says, "So when He heard that Lazarus was ill, he stayed two days longer in the place where He was." That doesn't seem to track. He loved Lazarus and his sisters, Mary and Martha. He had stayed in their home on many occasions. Yet, on hearing of his friend's illness, he did not go. He delayed for two whole days. It is difficult to perceive the meaning of that, and I can't explain it, except that I too have experienced the silences of God, as I am sure you have. A relationship of love is a relationship of trust. Humanly speaking, a trust relationship means sending your beloved off alone from time to time, confident he or she will be faithful. Perhaps in the same way, God sends us off alone, or apparently so. We do not feel his presence and our passionate prayers seem to go unheard. Nevertheless, he wants us to trust him. He wants to trust us. The silences of God are a mystery, and yet one of the dimensions of his love.

In discussing Lazarus' plight with the disciples, Jesus tells them Lazarus has fallen asleep. That may be the source of all those hokey sympathy cards with a similar message: "He is not dead, he is just away," or "He is just asleep." When the disciples misunderstand, Jesus finally tells them plainly that Lazarus is dead. Next he proposes that they go to him. The disciples try to talk him out of such a plan, reminding him that the temple leaders are out to kill him, and that it is a dangerous place to be. Of course, Jesus is determined to go, and, to their credit, they agree to go as well, even if it means dying with Him. The exchange points up that Jesus, in his love for us, will go anywhere. No place is off limits. As the Apostles' Creed points out, "He descended into hell." There is no hell that any of us can endure to which Jesus does not have access.

As he nears the village, Martha comes to meet him with a rebuke. "Lord, if you had been here, my brother would not have died" (John 11:21, RSV). A little later, Mary says the very same thing, letting Jesus know he has let them down. Haven't we all done that? How hard to accept the death of someone we love without feeling, "Lord, you could have prevented it. Why didn't you?"

I was a teenager in the army when I got the news that my father was very ill following surgery. I got an emergency furlough and arrived in Chicago at four o'clock in the morning after a thirty-hour train trip from Fort Bragg, North Carolina. I was too late. My father had died just three hours earlier. I still remember that anguished feeling. "Lord, why couldn't you have kept him alive for three more hours?"

When Martha remonstrates with the Master, he responds with those immortal words, "I am the resurrection and the life. Whoever lives and believes in me shall never die." He puts the question to her directly. "Do you believe this?" Her answer seems more general. "I believe that you are the Christ, the Son of God." Asked about life after death, we sometimes prefer more general answers. "I believe the Bible is the Word of God." "I believe that God is love." Faced with our own death and the death of a loved one, we need the assurance that he is the Lord of life and death.

At the tomb, "Jesus wept," words familiar even to non-scholars because they comprise the shortest verse in the Bible. We might wonder why he wept, in light of the events that followed. It would indicate that tears are appropriate for those left behind who are grieving. Our lives are diminished because our loved one is no longer with us. In weeping, Jesus, who became flesh, faced the pain and separation of death, just as we do.

The tomb was a cave, with a stone lain upon it, and Jesus ordered that stone removed. Martha, the eternal housekeeper, was dismayed. She protested, "Lord, by this time there will be an odor." I'm sure everything had been swept clean in preparation for the funeral party. The smell would cast a pall on things. Dear Martha, always mindful of the practical details. Jesus, unperturbed, uttered a short prayer and cried out, "Lazarus, come out!" This man, who had been dead for four days, wrapped like a mummy in his graveclothes, stumbled out of that tomb.

It's a powerful demonstration that with God there are no hopeless cases. Whatever your problem, drugs, alcohol, sex, financial disaster, relational difficulties, you can take courage. We worship a Lord who raised the dead, four days in the grave and rotting. We can invision Lazarus, coming out, trembling, blinking in the light, movements confined by the graveclothes. Jesus tells those standing around that the next step is theirs. "Unbind him and let him go." Lazarus is alive, but he can't move or talk. We are still called to that unbinding ministry with those men or women paralyzed by fears, guilt, compulsory behavior, or negative attitudes. Jesus raises the dead, but he has given us the power to unbind.

In facing death, we have an opportunity to face life in a whole new way. Start by living it to the hilt. Have no unfinished business in your life. If you are tortured with shameful secrets, confess them. If you have done something dishonest, make restitution. If there is someone you have offended, apologize. If there is someone you love and you have never been able to tell them, tell them now. If there is some adventure you want to begin with the Lord, start today. The life of adventure Jesus came to give us is available at any time and we can live it to the hilt until death comes.

Davis Willis, of the Funeral Association of America, reported on a survey which revealed that most Americans are death-avoiders. Thirty-five percent of us refuse to think about our own death. If we cannot accept our own eventual death, we cannot live. Malcolm Muggeridge tells of traveling in Ireland and passing an old lady sitting on the front stoop of her thatched cottage. "Pardon me, madam, what are you doing?" he asked. "I am learning how to die," was her reply. It's a startling thought. All of life is preparation for death. And when you realize that, you can begin to live.

I made a hospital call on a parishioner just before her death last year, and we were able to talk about her situation. She said, "It's a little untimely. I would like to have lived a little longer, but I am facing it." We prayed together, and I was about to leave when she made an unusual request. "Would you come over here and feel my hair?" I did so. "You know, before chemotherapy my hair was white. It's now come in black. All my life I've had straight hair, and wished it was otherwise. This new growth of hair is curly. Isn't the Lord good? I'm going to die with black, curly hair." I left that room deeply moved. My friend would die, but she was dying unafraid and full of thanksgiving to God.

But she is rare. Some beautiful lines from "The Rose" by Amanda McBroom sum up what is too often the human experience.

It's the heart afraid of breaking that never learns to dance.
It's the dream afraid of waking that never takes a chance.
It's the one who won't be taken who cannot seem to give.
And the soul afraid of dying that never learns to live.

The death process has often been compared to the birth process. Who of us would choose to leave a warm, comfortable womb and emerge into a cold and alien world? And yet we have the assurance of Jesus himself that there is a far better world on the other side of death. At the end of C. S. Lewis' *Chronicles of Narnia,* the four children are told by Aslan, the lion, that their parents have been killed in an accident. Aslan, who represents Jesus in this parable, says these words: "School is over. The holidays have begun. The dream is over, and now it is morning." At the end of those same chronicles, Lewis writes movingly to maintain that death is only the beginning of the real story, that death marks "chapter one of the great story which no one on earth has read; which goes on forever; in which every chapter is better than the one before."

One of the great souls of our time, Episcopal Bishop Warren Chandler, lay dying. An old friend sitting by his bedside asked him about his feelings. "Please tell me frankly, do you dread crossing the river of death?" "Why," Bishop Chandler replied, "My Father owns the land on both sides of the river. Why should I be afraid?"

8. The Fear of Hell

If you've lived in the real world for any length of time, someone has said to you, on more than one occasion, "Go to hell." When I hear that suggested to me or anyone else, I'm always tempted to follow up with some pertinent questions. "What do you mean? Why should I go there? How would I get there? How will I know when I've arrived? Who else will be there?" The phrase is among the most unpleasant things that one person can say to another. It conveys the desire to have something bad befall the other person—punishment, discomfort, even eternal demnation.

But I doubt that those who tell us to go to hell understand the true implications of the suggestion. In Luke's Gospel, Jesus spoke those very words to the devil. "Go to hell." They were appropriate to the situation, a command that he return to his place of origin. But we have good reason to think that the whole idea of hell is a joke for most people. Believers and nonbelievers can toss off a "go to hell" without a second thought. One cannot assume they believe there is such a place, or that they feel they have the power to send us there.

Christians cannot ignore the reality of hell. The Bible is full of references to such a place. In the sixteenth psalm, David thanks the Lord "for thou dost not give me up to Sheol or let thy Godly one see the pit" (Psalm 16:10, RSV). Jesus, in the twelfth chapter of Luke, warns us to "fear him who, after he has killed, has power to cast you into hell" (Luke 12:5, RSV). Children must have a hard time with this concept of hell, and Sunday School teachers tell me some of the difficulties they have in trying, for example, to describe it to a six-year-old. Nevertheless, even at that tender age, they have had experiences that represent some particular hell.

As kids, a good many of us have experienced some emotional hell at recess where we were ignored or persecuted. That so-called playtime can be the worst hour of the day, when you feel like the speckled bird on the playground. The divorce of one's parents is a hell at any age. But, for a six-year-old, security and certainty are blown away before any skills for coping or surviving are developed. The six-year-old may equate hell with those TV pictures of starving children in Ethiopia, with their great bellies and skinny arms and protruding eyes. Hunger and deprivation could certainly suggest hell at some level, as do the senseless violence and cruelty of far too many TV shows. Then again, hell can be an internal state. The comic strip "Bloom County" often features Binky's closet, a place from which that young lad's worst fears emerge at will, and all the demons of imagination take on reality.

Describing hell to a six-year-old is definitely a challenge, but it's almost as difficult to explain it to an adult. It has been tried through literature. Dante's inferno describes hell, its seven rings, and its occupants in great detail. The Faustian legend presents hell as a place inhabited by those who have bartered their souls for earthly rewards. In recent years a wild and wacky new comic strip entitled "Sylvia" has made its appearance, and it comments periodically on what the devil is thinking, or what we can expect in hell, such as that our sadistic third-grade teacher has been placed in charge.

Sartre, the secular existentialist, gave us his impression of hell in his play "No Exit." Three people are trapped in a room with no escape, and each one is suffering from unrequited love; the man loves the first woman, who loves the second woman, who loves the man. Certainly he has hit on what hell must feel like relationally. But the most brilliant book I know of on hell is the one mentioned in an earlier chapter, C. S. Lewis' *The Great Divorce.* Lewis' hell is a grey town, never clear, never raining. The citizens settle and resettle, always farther away from annoying neighbors. They are excluded from heaven by their own choice and by their inability to admit they were wrong in any way.

We have some biblical descriptions of both heaven and hell. Heaven has pearly gates and streets of gold. We don't take that literally, but rather as a kind of pictorial image helpful to people in a primitive age. Heaven may very well have pearly gates and streets of gold, but I think it will offer something more precious and more lasting than either of those. Hell, on the other hand, is supposedly a place with a lake of eternally burning fire. The early missionaries tried to explain that concept to the Eskimos, who thought it sounded great and wanted to know how to get there. I tend to believe that the lake of fire represents the fire of jealousy, ambition, or rage. Surely hell is that place where, by our own choice, we are consumed with self, our own appetites and ambitions.

As believers, we know that hell is as real a place as heaven. We don't know where heaven is. It may be a trillion light years from here, or it may be all around us in a dimension we can't presently discern. Hell may be a place within touching distance if we could move outside of our earthly time and space limitations. The temperature of hell, its scenery and architecture, are all matters for conjecture. The Bible doesn't give us details about those things. But we get a good deal more light in terms of its inhabitants.

Contrary to folklore, it is not a place for bad people. If that were true, we'd all be going there. Christians are not good people; they are forgiven people. We speak of those in hell as eternally damned, and yet the Apostles' Creed includes a belief that Jesus descended into hell. That makes me hopeful that there is, therefore, a way out. If our Redeemer was at one time there, then there must be a beachhead of grace and love and forgiveness. But I'm aware this puts me on shaky ground theologically.

We might well ask why a loving, omnipotent God would permit the existence of hell. One theory is that hell is a place of punishment for evil deeds, where those rotten people will finally get their comeuppance. But I prefer to think it is a place where God ceases to contend with us. If we have resisted his will and his way throughout life, he finally lets us have it our way. Whatever and wherever hell is, it is a place where God is not, and where darkness rules. It is a place where we are free to have it all our own way with all the other people who want to have it their own way. Even God cannot force his love on us.

Jesus came primarily, he tells us over and over again in scripture, to establish the Kingdom of God. He did not come merely to teach and heal, though he did those things. That Kingdom is the rule of God in the world, and it exists here and now. Those who have said yes to Jesus as Lord and Savior are a part of his Kingdom and are committed to extending his rule in the world. If that is so, then there must be a kingdom in opposition to that, a kingdom of darkness, made up of those who do not want the rule of God in their lives.

As we said, God cannot force his rule and his Kingdom on anyone. He is a gracious God. Those who reject him must congregate someplace where God is not. It is, in essence, the kingdom of self, and that's the commodity the devil deals in. He trades on our self-love and our ambition. He says, "Why don't you get yours and get it now? Take care of yourself. If you don't, nobody will. You deserve it. Take what you can, even if you have to use other people to get it."

Jesus speaks about those who kill the body. The body is all that is temporal, your physical life, this world, your time, money, and substance. All of that will pass away. We are not to worry about those who have the power to kill the body. That's going to go, in any event. We are not going to live forever. I say to the coffee addicts on my staff, "That stuff is going to kill you," and it is perfectly true. Given enough time, everything is going to kill us. Life is going to kill us. The body, with its comforts and pleasures, is temporal. The soul, our uniqueness, our personality, is eternal. Those who can persuade us to let go and indulge our self-centeredness and self-interest are the people to fear.

The alarming truth behind the concept of heaven and hell is that everybody lives forever. Jesus did not deliver us from death, but from hell. We all die, and when we do, life goes on in some form. That's the biblical message. The question is, what kind of life will be continued beyond the grave?

The idea of selling your soul seems an outmoded one, but I venture to guess there is something worse than hell for a lot of people, and to avoid that, they might be willing to jeopardize the soul. It may be a matter of instant gratification—casual sex, carousing, or a quick buck through some dishonest deal. On a more sophisticated level, we can sell our soul to the company store. That's what people did back in the old mining days in West Virginia. Workers were totally dependent upon the company and they owed the store as much as or more than they earned. They never got out of debt. There are corporations today who want your soul. They'll make you rich and successful if you are completely at their disposal. Your time is theirs, and you are moved about at will. Marriage and family are secondary to the commitment to the company.

What offer could the devil make you that might tempt you to give up your soul? We'd like to think we're not for sale, but the Prince of Darkness trades in some very valuable commodities. Most of us are striving for vocational success. If you are a musician, the chance to compose the greatest piece of music ever written, better than Mozart or Beethoven, might seem worth the loss of the soul. I've been writing books for over twenty years and if I had an offer to write the finest book in the world next to the Bible, it might be hard to turn down.

The devil has the power to offer profitable deals and powerful positions. In this age of preoccupation with physical beauty, some might consider giving up their soul for a perfect body or a perfect face, a perfect ten. Wealth alone may not be a temptation, but let's say there's a clause, just for Christians. You'll have billions to give to missions in exchange for your soul. You might want to think that one over. Would you trade your soul for really big stakes: to save your country? To cure cancer or AIDS?

One of my favorite movies is *A Man for All Seasons,* and I've seen the TV rerun any number of times. Near the end, Sir Thomas Moore is being tried for treason unjustly and illegally. One of the witnesses testifying against him is an old protegé and former friend. This man has agreed to lie about Moore's behavior and character and, in return, the king has made him the Exchequer of Wales. Having testified, he walks past the prisoner sitting in the dock, and Sir

Thomas notices his badge of office. He makes just one comment, something like this: "The Bible warns us about losing our souls to gain the whole world—but for Wales?"

Jesus addresses our fears specifically when he reminds us in that same chapter of Luke's Gospel that God cares about the sparrows. They are not spared from death, and neither are we. We will not be spared problems and misfortunes. Unfair things happen to all of us, but God knows and cares for us far more than he does for the sparrows. We are not to be anxious for our daily needs, but to "fear Him who has power to throw you into hell."

Hell, as we said, is not for the bad, nor heaven for the good. We have all sinned and fallen short of the glory of God (Romans 3:23, RSV). Hell may be for the people who think they are good, and heaven for those who know they're bad. But scripture is clear that heaven is for those willing to repent, willing to live in forgiveness by God's grace. It is for those wanting to live under God's rule, even though we fail from time to time. Atonement and redemption are difficult concepts to understand, but I read a story recently that tried to portray them in simple terms.

A little boy and his father were frolicking in the yard when a bee landed on the boy's cheek. The lad happened to be allergic to bees, and one sting could result in death. The father was in a panic. He didn't dare intervene or even yell, lest he startle the bee. A second or two later the bee took off, flew around, landed on the father's arm and stung him. The father laughed in relief. Bees have just one sting, and that bee could pose no further threat to his son.

Jesus has taken the sting out of death for us by his life and death and resurrection. He invites us to be a part of his Kingdom. In the words of the third verse of Luther's great hymn: "The body they may kill: God's truth abideth still. His Kingdom rules forever."

9. The Fear of Fear

Imagine if you will that you have been asked to take part in a research project. You live in a house with a detached garage, one about twenty-five feet from your back door. A one foot-wide I Beam, the kind used in building skyscrapers, will be placed between your back door and the garage, with sensors on both sides of it. Your assignment is to walk on that I Beam every time you go back and forth to your garage without stepping off the sides and activating the sensors. If you can do that successfully for one whole year, you will be given ten thousand dollars. Most of us would take that offer. I know I would.

You would probably walk that I Beam at least twice a day with total success, frequently carrying groceries, babies, or sports equipment. At the end of the year, you get your check, but you are then given an opportunity to make a second ten thousand dollars. That I Beam is going to be placed on the fiftieth floor of a skyscraper under construction. You have only to do once what you have already done flawlessly at least seven hundred times—walk those same twenty-five feet. I wouldn't touch an offer like that, and I doubt that many of us would. A whole new dimension has been added to a simple act that we have succeeded in at least seven hundred times.

In earlier chapters, we have talked about any number of fears, most of them based on facts. Somewhere out there is something tangible and scary. But a lot of fear is not rational, not explainable. We are simply afraid of being afraid. In a speech geared to reassure a nation in the midst of war, President Franklin Roosevelt used that famous phrase, "We have nothing to fear but fear itself." It was a timely statement, urging people not to give in to hysteria. Determination and a unified national effort were required.

We discussed in an earlier chapter the biblical account of a storm at sea and the fear the disciples experienced. But there is a second sea story in Matthew's Gospel in which the disciples are caught in turbulent winds and waves and Jesus is not present. If you've been in a small boat in stormy seas, it is terrifying, and fear is justified. When a figure approaches, looking like a ghost, the disciples are full of fear. That seems logical. As the ghost approaches, claiming to be their master, Peter is doubtful and wants proof. He calls out, "Lord, if it's you, bid me come to you on the water" (Matt. 14:28 RSV). Peter, the fisherman, the seaman, has never seen anyone walk on water, but he knows his Master is capable of miracles, and he wants to test his own powers over the natural laws. He needs Jesus to reassure him that he can do it, that he can actually get out of the boat and walk on the surface of the sea.

Jesus does tell Peter to come, and I can just picture that scene—Peter slipping off his sandals, hitching up his robe and climbing out over the gunwales. At the height of the storm, he leaves the boat and starts to walk toward Jesus. I'm sure he was experiencing a host of emotions, and it has to have been an almost mystical experience in which he was mesmerized by the power of the Lord. I'm sure he is delighted with himself and his new prowess, kind of a "Look Ma, no hands" attitude. He may even feel some pride that only he has taken the initiative and tried this stunt, demonstrating a degree of faith and courage lacking in the other eleven.

Peter's euphoria is short-lived. He looks around and realizes the improbability of the situation, and panics. In the midst of wind and waves, he is actually walking on water. Instantly, he starts to sink and cries out in fear. We are not sure of the source of Peter's fears. Does he suddenly panic at being in an inappropriate place, doing an impossible thing? His success is undermined by the fear that it won't last. He is afraid of being afraid. "Save me," he cries out.

Immediately, Jesus reaches out his hand, and how foolish Peter must feel at that moment. All his delight in his new powers vanish as he receives a rebuke from Jesus. According to the text, it is "Oh man of little faith, why did you doubt?" (Matt. 14:31, RSV). Peter is beaten by an unworthy foe—his own fear. There are a lot of things out there to be afraid of, then and now. Let's not be beaten by our own fear. Jesus seems to be saying, "Peter, is that all I can expect from you?"

The moment Jesus and Peter step over the gunwale and back into the boat, the wind ceases and, "they were amazed. They worshipped him." Jesus could just as well have calmed the storm earlier, to make walking on the water easier, but he did not. The storm continued. Most of us have been buffeted by winds and waves more than once in our lives. Jesus does not always calm the storm, but he is with us in it, and we have to trust that he is. We may even be called on to leave the boat in the midst of the storm.

The fear of fear is a destructive emotion which erodes our confidence and courage, and for most of us, it is omnipresent. There are a few brave souls who would take that ten thousand dollars and walk the I Beam on the fiftieth floor with no problem. The rest of us are terrified just by the thought of such a feat. However, in dealing with the fear of fear, there are a couple of strategies that are commonly employed.

First of all, we can simply avoid the fearful. We can resolve never to be in a place where we might fail. We're never going to try to walk on the water. We're going to build a safe life, a life without fear. I don't advise that course. We may try to get through life armed with every conceivable remedy to combat problems. We arm ourselves with road maps and travelers' checks, aspirins and mouthwashes, raincoats and umbrellas, flares and parachutes. Every contingency is provided for. We never go anyplace unless it's safe or unless it can be made safe.

Secondly, we can look for the magic potion to remove fear. There is no shortage of those—tranquilizers, sleeping pills, and alcohol are some of the obvious ones. But sometimes we seek safety in a relationship. We put all of our emotional eggs in one basket—the perfect spouse, parent, or child. Marriage is seen as the way to a blissful, problem-free future. A longed-for child is supposed to bring us total fulfillment.

I'd suggest a third strategy for dealing with this fear of fears, and that is to grab it by the throat and wrestle it to the ground. One exponent of this radical approach is Hugh Downs, the TV commentator. At 67, he drives a Formula A racing car, he is a glider pilot, he goes scuba diving along the Great Barrier Reef in Australia. He has ridden a killer whale bareback. He was almost washed overboard while sailing from Panama to Tahiti. During an expedition to the South Pole, he helped pull to safety a man who had fallen down a crevasse.

Asked in an interview about these exploits, he replied that he savors the feel, taste, and smell of danger. The facing and conquering of fear is to a large extent what drives him. "It's something I've had to deal with all my life," he confesses. "I was always full of fear. First, I was a terribly timid child. When I started out in radio I had a murderous case of mike fright, and then, on television, camera fright. I discovered that there's only one way to handle fear—go out and scare yourself to death."

I met a professional wrestler some years ago with that same philosophy. He was giving his witness at a conference, and he was wearing a big, pink, fuzzy sweater. If you are his size, you can get away with wearing a big, pink, fuzzy sweater. He told of being a timid, frightened child. "What changed my life was a sermon I heard in my church. 'Do the thing you fear the most, and the death of fear is certain.' I was scared of physical combat, so I began to lift weights and, eventually, to wrestle."

How do we deal with this fear of fear from the faith perspective? There are some strategies that you and I as Christians can tap into that will see us through the storms. I can think of at least three.

First of all, test the Lord. That's what Peter did. He did something outrageous. He walked on the water for at least a few moments. We need to ask for and expect a tough assignment, instead of saying, "Lord, why me? I've had enough." Say instead, "Lord, where do you want me? Help me to climb over the side of the boat and walk to you." G. K. Chesterton said, "An adventure is only an inconvenience rightly considered." Dorothy Parker, secular writer, said, "They sicken of the calm who know the storm." You and I were bred for the storm. Life is at its best when the storm is raging.

A policeman friend in a distant city once told me about a place in the station house called the "Give Up Room." When the detectives and policemen get weary of chasing criminals and are feeling scared of heading out once more into those dangerous streets, they go to that room to relax and drink coffee and wait for the criminal to come in and give himself up, which, of course, is highly unlikely. I wonder how many salesmen have a "Give Up Room" where they can go when they're feeling tired or timid, a place to drink coffee and wait for customers to seek them out and buy their products. It's easy to resort to the "Give Up Room" in any tough situation, but by God's grace we can ask for tough assignments and expect his help in them.

Secondly, trust the Lord. Act as if you are going to succeed, and believe that God wants you to succeed. Don't trust your feelings. A fifty-six-year-old man named Arnold Lemerand was walking down the street when he heard some children screaming. Running to the source of the commotion, he found a group of kids, one of whom was trapped under a huge cast-iron pipe which had rolled off an embankment. Without hesitation, he hoisted that pipe and released the child. The pipe turned out to weigh eighteen hundred pounds, and Mr. Lemerand had tried to avoid heavy lifting since his heart attack six years earlier. When he attempted to lift that same pipe a second time, he could not. The point is, he did something no normal person could do, simply because he was there and he tried. We all tend to be so aware of our limitations that we limit our potential.

A hundred years ago, the YWCA trained eight young women in the use of a brand new machine—the typewriter. Those in charge of the program were concerned about the effect this machine would have on supposedly frail and delicate women. Physicians were called in to administer physical and mental tests to determine if these recruits would be able to endure the pressures of typing. It was feared that their minds would snap with the effort of mastering this new machine. At that time, machines were considered the strict province of men. Women's talents and capacities were supposed to be limited. It seems ludicrous, but we can go through life with those same archaic ideas of our own potential.

I am nervous and fearful about preaching, even though I do it almost every Sunday. It's still terrifying. After more than thirty years, it doesn't get any better. Saturday night is largely sleepless and usually accompanied by intestinal upset. Nevertheless, I love preaching, and I don't plan to quit. I face that fear weekly and, with God's help, I conquer it.

Third, keep your eyes on Jesus. That's what Peter did not do. When you are walking on the water any time, any place, keep your eye on Jesus. If you focus on the storm, you are sure to sink. Our human nature feeds us lines like, "What am I doing here? I'm in over my head." We need to keep our eyes on Jesus who bids us come and who can enable us to accomplish the improbable.

A daily devotional is one important way of keeping our eyes on Jesus. When we read the Bible and pray, we are focusing on him and his powers and not on the problems of the day. The trick in walking that I Beam fifty stories up is to avoid looking down.

If you are a circus buff, like me, you know about Karl Wallenda, the patriarch of the Flying Wallendas clan, the greatest high-wire artists in circus history. Karl Wallenda died performing in 1978, and his wife had some unusual comments on that sad occurrence. "All Karl thought about for three straight months prior to his accident was falling. It was the first time he had ever thought about that, and it seemed to me that he put all of his energies into not falling, rather than walking the tightrope." There's a lesson there.

Rather than focus on failure or on our fears, keep our eyes on Jesus. As the Apostle Paul wrote, "I can do all things through Christ who strengthens me."

My old friend, Lloyd Ogilvie, had a terrible accident a few summers ago in Scotland. A bad fall destroyed his left leg and knee and even a piece of his hip. His Los Angeles doctor performed multiple operations to correct the damage, and he was ordered not to stand on that leg for three months. "If you do," said his doctor, "I'm through with you. You will destroy all of the work we have done." Lloyd spent three months in a wheelchair with the leg propped up, in constant pain. At the end of that time, the doctor checked him out and gave him entirely new advice. "Lloyd, I want you to stand on that left leg with all your weight. If it breaks down, I can fix it."

Those times come for all of us when we are required to rest our full weight on some faith venture, climb out of the boat, and walk on the water. Welcome those challenges. They are the means, perhaps the only means, by which we can put to rest that fear of fear.

10. The Fear of the Unknown

Fear of the unknown may not be as universal as some of the fears we have been discussing, but it is a fear that affects many of us. It is perhaps most commonly focused on our eventual death; on when and how that will occur. Fortunately, few of us have any foreknowledge about that. Even if we are lucky enough to live a long time, we may fear the mental and physical debilitation that almost always accompanies old age. None of us looks forward to what may prove to be a time of helplessness and dependency.

A nurse in a care facility for senior citizens said recently, "Sometimes as I am getting an older female patient ready for bed, it occurs to me that she might have once gone to sleep between satin sheets, wearing silk pajamas. Now she wears a double diaper. These are not the golden years but the rusting years." Those fears of old age are compounded by the threat of loneliness. Will there be anyone left at the end to love me, or even care about me?

On the other hand, your fear of the unknown may be activated by a present problem. You might be facing a job change or a job loss. Some difficult family circumstance may seem to have no terminal point, and no promise of a happy ending. Fears might center in uncertainty about financial matters. Will we have enough resources to pay the bills—or to retire with some measure of security? A recent cartoon pictured a bearded man dressed in a long robe, carrying a sandwich board which proclaimed, "Repent! The World

Will Never End." A bystander is saying to his companion, "Now *that* scares me!" That speaks to some of us. This mess we're in right now may never end, and we're not sure we can endure it any longer.

Some years ago, I read about a judge in Yugoslavia who had an unfortunate accident. He was electrocuted when he reached up to turn on the light while standing in the bathtub. His wife found his body sprawled on the bathroom floor. He was pronounced dead and, as was the custom in that particular town, he was placed in a room under a crypt in the town cemetery for twenty-four hours before burial. In the middle of the night, the judge came to, realized where he was, and rushed over to alert the guard, who promptly ran off, terrified.

Fortunately, he returned with a friend, and they released the newly-revived judge. His first thought was to phone his wife and reassure her. He got no farther than, "Darling—it's me," when she screamed and fainted. Next he went to the houses of several friends, who were sure he was a ghost. In a last, desperate measure, he called a friend in a distant city, who had not heard of his death, and who interceded for him with his family and friends and vouched for his apparent resurrection.

We can appreciate the initial reaction to that miraculous revival. Faced with the unknown, with circumstances that are beyond our experience, we respond with disbelief. Even the disciples, who had some clear evidence of Jesus' unusual powers, were often frightened by the signs and wonders he performed during his three-year ministry. We need to remember that our God, according to the biblical record, is a God of the unexpected. Who would have predicted that God would instruct Noah to build a boat and round up all those animals in order to save a righteous remnant from the flood? Who would have expected that the waters of a great sea would part to make a path for the Israelites, only to close again over the pursuing army? The citizens of Jericho must have gotten accustomed to having that horde of Israelites marching around their city, day after day, in silence. They never expected that one of those days, trumpet blasts would bring their walls crashing down and they would be conquered. Mary and Martha, preparing their beloved brother for burial, never expected that he would emerge from his tomb just three days later. The women at the tomb that first Easter morning were astounded by what they found, and their reports of the resurrection were at first disbelieved.

The biblical narrative is full of the unexpected. So many incidents do not follow any known pattern. Men and women of faith through the ages have had a hard time adjusting to God's radical intervention in their lives. No wonder that the church and its people have a hard time with change. I discussed this problem with one of our elders recently. He is someone who adapts to personal change fairly readily, but he is very cautious about any new direction for the church. Each suggestion is met with a negative response. "Wait a minute. Let's go slowly here." We've all heard the seven last words of the church: "We never did it like that before." But, historically and biblically, God is always doing something new with his people.

I like to shake my congregation up occasionally with some drastic proposals. Why not, for instance, sell all our buildings, give the money to some famine relief agency, and go rent space downtown? We could start with a clean slate in terms of finding God's will for this part of his family. Let's find out if we could still minister as effectively without this familiar building, to which so many have a sentimental attachment. That would be a leap into the unknown for our parish, one they're not quite ready for.

Most of our institutions are functioning along fairly predictable lines, the church included, and it takes some cataclysmic circumstance to bring about directional changes. Our personal lives are, for the most part, more fragile. We may be faced with the unknown at any time. The market crash of 1987 gave us all a new awareness of the tenuousness of our financial fortunes. Financial losses, borne stoically or even cheerfully by some, can cast others into complete despair and, in extreme cases, prompt suicide. The loss of a job makes us come to grips with our fear of the unknown, as does the erosion of our health.

We have a group in our church for the visually impaired. Some are already blind and others are dealing with severely diminished sight. I met with them last month and shared my own problem. I have glaucoma. My sight is already slightly impaired. It may get worse, and it may not. The future is unknown. They welcomed me in a whole new way once I had become one of them. So many of them have demonstrated that you can be a whole, alive, saint of God, even without sight.

Other members of our church family are seriously handicapped physically. The fact that most of them are making it triumphantly gives the rest of us hope. The fear of diminished physical capacity is a reality for all of us at any age, and perhaps its most pernicious aspect is that its consequences are unknown, unimagineable.

Entering into a marriage relationship requires embarking on an unknown course. Will you live happily ever after? Will you end up among the depressing divorce statistics? One of you is probably going to die before the other, leaving the survivor alone and bereaved. The future may hold sudden fame or sudden ignominy.

A lottery winner is immediately plummeted into wealth and notoriety, but our fortunes can take a downward turn just as unexpectedly. A next-door neighbor in Florida had been for many years the president of a Canadian bank. He habitually received at least five hundred Christmas cards each year. The Christmas after his retirement to Florida, he received ten. It was a devastating awakening.

Sometimes we are propelled into the unknown with a clear sense of God's leading. One of our parishioners shared a story like that with me. He met his wife in a Hebrew class in Israel. He was not a Christian, and she was. Within two weeks, he had become both a believer and a bridegroom. He says, "For those early weeks I felt I had practically no choice. My decisions were all automatic." There are times in your life and mine when God has us in his grip, and we are seemingly just being moved along. It seems impossible to veer off course.

But the going can get tough even when we sense God's clear leading. That happened to the disciples. In the last chapter, we discussed the storm at sea, during which Jesus appears to them walking on the water. The storm is so severe that they are in danger of sinking, and yet Jesus has directed them to get in that boat and cross the lake. When he comes to help, walking on the waves, their reaction is a little surprising. They don't say, "It's an angel," or, "It must be the Master." They are certain they are seeing a ghost.

The disciples, who have witnessed the abundance of Jesus' power, seem particularly slow to understand. They have, after all, just seen the feeding of the five thousand. Jesus had been teaching all morning, and people were getting hungry. The disciples started to be anxious, as usual. "How will we feed this mob?" "Don't worry," they were told. A few loaves and a few fish were found. When they were blessed and passed out, they provided food for the whole throng. Nevertheless, just a few hours later, when Jesus once again comes to the rescue, they are afraid. They seem to have missed the message that at the heart of the universe, there is a friend who is on their side and who is eager to bless them. If we have trusted God we can welcome even the unknown. Paul spells it out for us. "All things work together for good to them that love the Lord" (Romans 8:28).

My wife had an operation on her knee a few years ago. Before surgery, the doctor asked her to assume the fetal position, so that he could administer a local anaesthetic. In the course of the surgery, she was asked, "Do you know what position your legs are in?" "They're drawn up," she replied. "No," she was told, "actually, they are perfectly straight out on the operating table." The last message her mind had gotten was that her legs were in a particular position. That's our problem as we face the unknown. The mind gives us a message of fear, and we assume a position of fear, even when the circumstances are not particularly frightening.

The unknown is always coming at us in new forms and new shapes, but we need not meet it with the old attitudes of pessimism or dread. One of my most life-changing experiences happened on a cruise to the Holy Land. Our daughter and her college roommate were along, and the ship stopped at Dubrovnik, Yugoslavia. On our return to the boat, all the passengers were present, except for our daughter and her roommate. In a communist country, you all sail, or nobody sails; so we couldn't leave. The ship's first mate and I got into a cab and set out to find the girls. Driving into the city I shared my concern. "Friend," I said, "something is very wrong here. These are highly intelligent, very responsible young women. They have got to be sick or kidnapped or run over by a truck." The first mate turned to me with a steely glance. "Mister," he said in his Greek accent, "I don't know what business you're in, but let me give you some advice. Always believe the best first." Of course, the two girls did turn up. They had not adjusted their clocks to shore time, and therefore were one hour late. But my mind was in a position of fear and anticipating the worst.

I often think with awe of those early explorers, setting out in tiny boats, across treacherous seas, with few if any navigational aids. For the most part, they set their course by the stars, those signs eternal in the heavens. You and I face the unknown every day of our lives in some dimension. We can only trust in that unwavering absolute, our omnipotent, omniscient, omnipresent God.

You have probably read about Thor Heyerdahl, the man who built and sailed the Kontiki to recreate the journey he believed the Egyptians had made across the Atlantic to South America. He had some interesting comments to make on the perils of that voyage. All the dangers lie along the shoreline with its reefs and shoals, according to Heyerdahl. Leaving that for the expanse of the ocean brought a great sense of relief.

So, in our lives, we may be more at risk hugging the safety of the shore: vocationally, relationally or in any other area. The unknown perils are more numerous there than in the vast expanse of God's wider opportunities and challenges.

III. FACING OUR FEARS

11. Facing Pain

I'm sure there is no human being who has not experienced some degree of pain. Certainly pain is not distributed evenly. Some have suffered intense pain, perhaps over a long period. For others it comes intermittently and ranges from mild to extreme. In one sense, I'm not particularly qualified to write about pain. I have had an unusually healthy life. I have never been hospitalized for any reason. I have not had a child die, nor watched one suffer from severe illness, or mental or physical handicaps. I have not been through a divorce, which friends tell me is a process in which one feels all the grief and loss of a death.

Nevertheless, I have experienced pain, some physical but most of it psychic. Perhaps the most exquisite emotional pain comes from loving someone, opening your heart and mind to that person, and being rejected or betrayed. That has happened to me with close sisters and brothers in the faith, and that has been and is the source of some of my most acute pain.

The wonder is that the feeling of pain cannot be stored in our memory banks. God has made it so. You may recall having felt it, but you cannot relive it. It's gone. Yet the fear of that pain recurring, and the determination to avoid it at any cost can paralyze us.

Christian Scientists say that there is no pain. It is not real. But that kind of denial seems a poor strategy for handling the reality of pain. A little limerick I heard years ago goes to the heart of the matter:

There was a faith healer of Beal
Who said, "Although pain isn't real,
When I sit on a pin
And it punctures my skin,
I dislike what I fancy I feel."

In almost every one of its sixty-six books, the Bible reinforces the belief that pain is real, and, furthermore, a part of life here on earth. On the cross, Jesus experienced most of the kinds of pain that you and I can face. His pain was beyond words and is summed up with stark simplicity in Mark's gospel with "And they crucified Him" (Mark 15:24, RSV). There is no further description. Medical people tell us it is the cruelest form of death, producing unbelievable physical suffering.

Only slaves and the basest of criminals were so executed, which tells us that Jesus also experienced social pain. He was put in a place of ignominy between two despised criminals. Part of the tragedy of the homeless of our time, whose numbers are increasing in the land, is the social pain associated with their state. Not only have they no shelter in which to be warm and dry, they have no place in our industrious, profit-motivated society. They are the outcasts, the disenfranchised.

Jesus experienced the pain of humiliation. People walking by mocked him. Most of us have firsthand knowledge of that kind of pain. We still remember those traumatic moments, especially as children, when our peers bullied us, teased us, or worse. A good many of us know what it's like to be the wallflower at the dance, or the last one chosen for the team, with all the attendant taunting and cruelty. Humiliation before your peers produces a special kind of pain, one Jesus went through.

He endured professional humiliation as well. Jesus, the Messiah, Lord of the church and creation, was helpless. And the jeers must have wounded him. "Look at him. He saved others. He can't even save himself." And remember, all this took place in front of Jesus' intimate friends, his mother, and his brothers, and in the company of women who had traveled with him. Humiliation before our parents is especially hard for some of us. We live our whole lives trying to please Mom and Dad, often with little success. We never could become what they wanted us to be, and we can even go to the grave burdened by those regrets. "Sorry, Mom, Dad, I tried to do more, be more."

But in addition to all the physical and social pain, the personal and professional humiliation, Jesus experienced spiritual pain. He cried in Aramaic, *"E'lo-i, E'lo-i, la'ma sabach-tha'ni?"* (Mark 15:34, RSV). From his total humanity, he berated God as you and I have done, "My God, my God, why hast thou forsaken me?" Our phrase is more likely to be, "God, why me? Where are you when I need you?" Jesus knew the spiritual pain of feeling all alone in creation, deserted even by his Father in heaven. He understands those times when we go through that particular kind of pain.

Some vindication eventually comes. Seeing how he died, the Roman centurion said, "Surely, this was the Son of God." Jesus was already dead and didn't hear that. The biblical narrative seems to specialize in people who are vindicated after their death. God promised Abraham he would father a great nation, and he produced one legitimate heir. The Promised Land was taken by the Israelites only after the death of their leader, Moses, who had given forty years of his life and leadership to that goal. Vindication may arrive too late for any of us.

Any and all of the kinds of pain we are discussing can be separated into two basic categories: avoidable pain and unavoidable pain. In that first category is the pain that is the result of unhealthy choices. If you have had to deal with someone suffering from a hangover, you know how hard it is to feel sorry for that person. That pain, however acute, is the result of dumb behavior the night before. Indigestion is in a similar category. You head for the Alka Seltzer because you have eaten unwisely or unrestrainedly. Someone has said, "I approve of fast food places hiring senior citizens. When I order a chiliburger with onions and barbecue sauce, I prefer to get it from someone who's had a little experience with indigestion." If you are in physical pain from drinking, smoking, overeating, or physical inactivity; from drugs, improper diet, or even sexual promiscuity, don't expect a lot of sympathy. You are reaping the consequences of irresponsible behaviour.

But the world seems full of undeserved pain, unjust pain. There are birth defects and crippling injuries as a result of accidents. There is the pain of poverty and hunger. The pain of disease is especially frustrating in Third World countries where epidemics go unchecked for lack of drugs or medical care, or because of government policies.

Let's remember, however, that physical pain, for the most part, whether it is deserved or undeserved, serves a purpose. It is a gift given to preserve and protect life. I read about two children in London born with a congenital insensitivity to pain. The four-year-old boy is jealous of his year-old sister. He stabs her, punches her, even burns her, and all the while she lies there smiling. Oblivious to his own pain, he does bizarre things; jumps out of windows, runs on a broken ankle. These children cannot live long with this deficiency, and their parents are distraught. It is pain that makes us get treatment, protect an injured limb, see the doctor or the dentist.

We parents try to rescue our children from pain, and sometimes, in the case of emotional or relational pain, we do them a disservice. Pain can cause us to make healthier, more positive choices in the future. Most families of alcoholics have been rescuing the addict for far too long. Until alcoholics experience the consequences of their addiction, however extreme, they will have no strong motivation to change.

A boyhood friend and I once found a Monarch butterfly cocoon. We took it to his house to watch it develop. When the insect began to come out of the cocoon, it seemed to be having a difficult struggle. Finally, my friend, who fancied himself a young scientist, took a scissor and snipped the cocoon in order to simplify the procedure. Out came a great bloated body and two tiny wings. That Monarch butterfly never flew. It walked around with that bloated body and those shrunken wings all its remaining days. God designed that creature so that the struggle required to emerge releases the fluid from the body into the wings. That act of kindness, the snipping of the cocoon, destroyed the moth's ability to fly. It's a story to remember whenever we're tempted to rescue someone from their pain. Perhaps they need to discover the meaning and message of that pain.

Pain and love are bound together in some mysterious way. I can't explain it. We occasionally think to ourselves, "If I were God, I'd see to it that there would be no more pain." But we have to conclude that pain serves some ultimate purpose. In the opening paragraphs of John's Gospel we read, "The Word became flesh and dwelt among us" (John 1:14, RSV). Because of his love, God chose to enter our world and suffer. There was no other way to love his creation except through the pain of entering into it through his Son and sharing our life of pain.

Madeleine L'Engle in her book *Walking on Water* tells about an exchange between an ascetic rabbi and his disciple. "Rabbi," exclaimed the disciple, "I love you so much." The rabbi responded, "Do you know what hurts me, my son?" The disciple was puzzled. "I don't understand your question, rabbi. I am trying to tell you how much you mean to me, and you confuse me with irrelevant questions." "My question is neither confusing nor irrelevant," explained the rabbi, "for if you do not know what hurts me, how can you truly love me?" To love is to enter into someone else's pain and to be able to share your own pain.

In this matter of facing pain, let me make some things clear. If you are recovering from surgery, or are in constant pain with arthritis, or some other disease, thank God that somebody invented painkillers. But in facing the day-to-day pain of life, we do not need painkillers. Jesus faced all the kinds of pain we've already explored on that cross at Golgotha, but he refused a painkiller. "They offered him wine to drink mingled with gall, but when he tasted it He would not drink it" (Matt. 27:34, RSV).

Gestalt psychologists tell us to go into the pain. If you run from it or try to avoid it, fear of the pain will destroy you. Baron Von Hugel said, "Christianity gave to souls a faith and strength to grasp life's nettles." Life certainly has nettles, and they hurt. To live is to love, and love is costly and never entirely without pain.

Bob Schuller of the Hour of Power ministry was speaking in Korea, accompanied by his wife, Arvella, when they got tragic news. Their teenage daughter had been in a motorcycle accident and would need to have her leg amputated. They immediately made plans to fly home. Bob tells of sitting on that homeward-bound plane contemplating this hideous turn of events, when he was suddenly overwhelmed with tears. To avoid making a public display, he ran for the lavatory and did his sobbing behind locked doors. "Then," he says, "I began to remember hearing the Korean Christians singing 'Hallelujah, Hallelujah,' and I began to sing in the washroom at the top of my voice, 'Hallelujah, Hallelujah.' " How do you handle the pain of a teenage daughter about to lose her leg? You can order a double Scotch and try to dull the pain; you can head for the bathroom and seek God's own presence and comfort. Our ability to handle emotional, psychic pain in positive ways is one mark of our maturity as Christians.

Keep in mind, the purpose of life is not freedom from pain. If you had enough money to hire medical people to keep you comatose, drugged, and fed intravenously, you could go through the rest of your life never having to feel pain. But that's hardly living. The purpose of life, according to Jesus' words, is to love God with your whole heart, soul, mind, and strength, and to love your neighbor as yourself. That means loving a world full of people who are desperate for love, starting in your home or neighborhood. Do that and you will experience pain, I promise you.

A friend wrote me about a couple she knew in Alaska. The man, an elder in his church, divorced his wife three years ago and moved away. This past Christmas he called his ex-wife to tell her he was moving back to Alaska. "Do you know what that means?" he asked. She said, "No, what does that mean?" "Reconciliation," he said. "I no longer want to be in God's permissive will. I want to be in his perfect will. I'm not sure I love you right now, but I think God can take care of that." That's grasping the nettle, embarking on a course of obedience and faithfulness and trusting God that love may return. Oddly enough, the New Testament writers nowhere suggest that love is the basis for marriage. Rather, marriage is the basis for love, and these two wounded people are willing to explore that theory.

We say often that the life of faith is a journey. But what kind of journey is it? Is it a journey from one luxury hotel to the next? If we think that and get stuck in the alley some night, then of course we take painkillers, drugs, alcohol, sex, anything to ease the pain. But the Christian life was never meant to be a journey from the Hilton to the Marriott. It's a journey through the wilderness. Sometimes we do arrive at a luxury hotel, but most of the time we're camping out. The point is, we're moving, we're on our way, and the accommodations aren't important. God's people do not get special treatment. They get a companion, *the* companion, who has promised never to leave or forsake us.

Look for a moment at this matter of pain from God's point of view. If God had wanted to avoid pain, there would be no people. We have been a problem ever since the Garden of Eden. We have been rejecting him, betraying him, ignoring him. We are a pain in the neck to God. Had God been unwilling to accept pain, there would be no relationship possible with his creation, and no redemption of it.

You may be saying, "That all sounds good, but you can't possibly know the pain I'm in right now." Of course I don't, but here's a word of hope. Some years ago in Death Valley, the lowest, hottest, driest place on our hemisphere, there were nineteen consecutive days of rain, an unprecedented occurrence. When that rain stopped, the desert bloomed. There were poppies, larkspur, columbine, buttercups, Indian paint brush, and more. Over one hundred different kinds of flowers sprang from that desert floor. They had been dormant for years and years until the coming of the rain.

You may be experiencing your personal valley of death right now. Don't try to avoid the pain in destructive ways. Believe instead that the rain will eventually fall, and the flowers of your life will begin to bloom.

12. Facing Illness

No examination of our primary fears would be complete without examining the fear that is linked with illness. My wife and I got some new insights into that just last year. She is one of six children, and the sister nearest her own age, the one with whom she had shared a bed all their growing-up years, died of bone cancer just months after the disease was diagnosed. The swift progression of her illness may have been caused as much by her fears as by her physical deterioration.

Our fear of illness can be as devastating as the illness itself. A recent letter from a parishioner confirms that. He wrote,

Starting in January, I have had a series of panic attacks in varying degrees of severity. Several have been to the point of simulating heart attacks, and in one instance, I was sent to the hospital in the ambulance. I have seen the inside of more doctors' offices and clinics this past year than in my entire life previously. It has been as if my body has been telling me, "That's it. We can't go on like this any more." . . . In the last year I have had three complete physical exams and numerous brief visits to a number of doctors, since obviously those pronouncing me healthy have been mistaken. I have been sure that I have either AIDS, heart failure, a stroke, mental illness, measles, herpes, cancer, brain tumor or whatever else happens to be in the news that night. I just can't seem to believe that I'm healthy, and, in a world where there are so many truly sick people, why can I not embrace the fact that I am in good health?

In a similar vein, a 1957 medical journal contains an account of a Mr. Wright, who was a patient with advanced lymphosarcoma. All treatments had become ineffective. Tumors the size of oranges littered his neck, armpits, groin, chest, and abdomen. His spleen and liver were grossly enlarged. The thoracic lymph duct was swollen closed, and one to two quarts of milky liquid had to be drained from his chest each day. He had to have oxygen to breathe and his only medication was a sedative to help him on his way. That year, a miracle drug came on the market which was hailed as a new cancer cure. The clinic where Mr. Wright had been treated had permission to use a limited supply of this new drug. When Mr. Wright asked to take it, he was told that it would only be given to patients who had three to six months to live. According to the doctors, Mr. Wright had just days.

However, Mr. Wright was so persistent that his doctor agreed to give him one injection. The next day, the tumors were shrunken to almost unrecognizable size, and all symptoms had left. In three or four days, Mr. Wright left the hospital, perfectly well. He resumed a normal life, which included flying his own plane, until he read a newspaper article debunking the new miracle drug. Before long, he was sick again: the tumors came back, and he was again on the verge of death.

The doctors decided on an unusual plan. They told Mr. Wright that they had a new and better miracle drug which was being tested, and that he would receive an injection of it. The "new drug" was distilled water and nothing else. The patient got well again, and the tumors shrunk once more. There seems only one explanation for what happened to Mr. Wright. His faith in the cure made him well, while his fears made him sick.

Stories like this seem to give new weight to the relationship between fear and illness, faith and healing. One of the
healing stories reported in the Gospels has always been of
special interest to me. It is the story about Peter's mother-in-
law. The facts are fairly simple. She has a diagnosable illness, a fever. Jesus comes to the house and goes to her
bedside. He takes her hand and instructs her to get up. The
fever immediately leaves her and, in proof of her healing,
she goes out to help serve the meal, probably some elabo-
rate dinner. I have often speculated on the possible drama
behind that incident, wondering what might have made her
sick and what caused her recovery.

First of all, a woman in New Testament times had no
power. She was dependent upon a man for her very existence. Peter's mother-in-law was probably a widow, since
she lived with her daughter and son-in-law. Her position
was fairly secure because her daughter had married a good,
hardworking man with his own fishing business. We can
imagine the reaction to the news that Peter is leaving to
follow Jesus. Can't you hear the dialogue?

"You're going to do what?"

"Follow Jesus, Mary's son, the carpenter."

"For how long?"

"I don't know."

"Who's going to run the business? Who's going to take
care of us?"

Peter's mother-in-law had lost control of the situation.
Unable to convince her son-in-law that he must stay and do
the responsible thing toward his wife and her mother, I can
well imagine that her distress made her really sick. She
probably met Jesus for the first time when he came to the
house, because women didn't go out in the marketplace
very often in those days. Our Lord, love incarnate, sat by

her bed and was concerned about her health and her troubles. The fever left her, and she got up and got to work. That's one possible scenario.

We are told, of course, that germs are the cause of illness, and yet germs are with us all the time. Can you imagine how many germs are floating around a packed theater or a football stadium? Yet most of us go home well. Those who get sick don't do so because of that roomful of germs. We get sick because of the breakdown in the amazing immune system God has given us. When it is working, we can stay healthy, even in the contagious ward. Germs may cause illness, but most of the time we are protected from them. When other emotional factors come into play—fear and stress, to name a couple—our bodies break down and germs invade us.

Beyond that, fear has a somewhat magnetic quality I can't quite explain, but after a long lifetime of observing myself and others, I am convinced we are drawn to the very thing we fear the most. Our fears exert power over us. They often turn into self-fulfilling prophecies. In my first parish I met with an ecumenical group of men, one of whom was a surgeon and Episcopalian. We were sharing fears over coffee one morning when he shared his. "I fear two things. I fear the loss of my skills as a surgeon, and I fear I will suffer from some condition whereby I will be unable to breathe. I have watched patients with that problem, and it is frightening."

In a year's time, Dr. Bill got both emphysema and arthritis. Forced to give up his practice, he took up painting and became a passably talented artist, whose works were publicly exhibited. Later, a stroke on his right side deprived him of the use of his right hand. He was undaunted. Though formerly right-handed, he started to paint with his left hand. I happen to have the first picture Dr. Bill ever painted with his left hand, a scene of his own garden along the banks of the Susquehanna River. I treasure it because it is a monument to one man's determination to be creative until the day he dies. Nevertheless, the peculiar aspect of this story is that this man of faith seemed to have a fatal attraction for the very things he feared.

Fear can also block or impede our recovery from illness. Norman Cousins, author of *Anatomy of an Illness* and lay teacher at the medical school of UCLA, lectured in our town a while back. He reiterated what he has said in his book, which is that many people die from their diagnosis, rather than their disease. He compared the process to the ancient one in which the witch doctor points the bone, and the hapless victim believes the diagnosis and dies of fear. All of which puts a terrible burden on present-day doctors. What to tell the patient, and when?

A well-known doctor has written about his victory over pain. He was suffering from chronic, disabling back problems. His hobbies were tennis and gardening, and he could no longer do either. He had been hospitalized many times, and was considering an operation for a degenerative disc. Just before the surgery he heard a still, small voice inside, saying, "Do you know what your problem is? You are full of fear and anxiety because you are carrying a grievance that you haven't forgiven." When he was able to drop that long-term resentment, his pain left. He is now living an active life again, with no limitations.

Love, as the Apostle Paul writes in his letter to the Corinthians, is the greatest force in the world. People who can give and receive love are the healthiest and happiest among us. Perfect love, which is God's own love, casts out fear. Faith requires trusting in that perfect love and ceasing to be anxious. Love is not a romantic feeling or a theological formula. Love resides in a person—the person of Jesus Christ.

How then do we face illness without fear, and rely on perfect love? Here are some suggestions, both biblical and practical.

First of all, be reconciled to your eventual death, and stop fearing it. Death is God's gift. Even Lazarus, raised from the dead after three days in the tomb, eventually died. Secondly, don't accept any terminal verdict, no matter who pronounces it. No wise doctor will predict how long you will live. Nobody knows that. Many forces are operating which can affect our physical condition. A good doctor will explain the straight facts about your illness, and offer both hope and the help of any available resources.

Doomsayers are not limited to the medical profession. A friend who was recovering from a hip replacement operation tells about getting into an elevator in a downtown Seattle building. She was limping badly and the other passenger, a sour-looking woman, said to her, "What's wrong with you?" "I've had a hip replacement," explained my friend, "and I'm facing a second one, and it's all very painful." "You must be a great sinner," her companion commented. "Yes, I am," responded my friend, "but fortunately I'm forgiven through Jesus Christ." That mistaken belief that sin is the cause of illness was prevalent even in Jesus' day. Sin is not the cause of illness. We're all sinners, but illness seems indiscriminate, falling on the just and the unjust.

I further suggest you start living generously. Dr. James House, epidemiologist at the University of Michigan, reports on a survey taken in Tecumseh, Michigan, over a ten-year period. Researchers found that regular volunteer work, more than any other activity, dramatically increased life expectancy and vitality. Before long, you may get this kind of prescription from your physician: "Exercise regularly, eat a well-balanced diet, and do something nice for someone." It is sound advice. Jesus told us that in saving our life we will lose it; in losing our life, we will save it.

Bumper stickers and T-shirts are sometimes a source of genuine folk wisdom. I met some college kids at a conference in Chicago wearing sweatshirts with an intriguing message. The front side said, "Live as if this were your last day on earth." There was a second message on the back. "Die knowing you will live forever." In his book *Love, Medicine and Miracles,* Bernie Segal tells of visiting terminally ill patients and giving them this advice: "Quit worrying about the electric bill and the leak in your roof and whether your kids are doing well. Let go. This may be the last day of your life." On the next morning's rounds he often finds some of them up and moving about and enjoying a big breakfast. The explanation? "I took your advice, doctor. I quit worrying." Why wait until the last day of your life to stop worrying? Stop now.

Finally, in facing illness, I advise you to live in abundance, not lack. We can be overwhelmed by fears simply because of the demands being made upon us by all the people we can't control in our lives—our spouse, parents, kids, business colleagues. If God's spirit lives in us, then we ought to have resources to meet those demands. We may be like Peter and John, responding to the beggar at the gate of the temple, "I have no silver and gold, but I give you what I have" (Acts 3:6, RSV). Begin to believe you have all the resources you will need for living today, tomorrow, and all your tomorrows, enough resources to meet all the demands made on you. Live rich.

One of our best-known twentieth-century missionaries was E. Stanley Jones. He had a call from Christ early on to go to India to convert the intellectuals. His mission was exceedingly successful, but he suffered a nervous breakdown in the process. He spent some time in the hills resting, then returned once again only to go through a second nervous breakdown. He was sent home. His third breakdown occurred while he was conducting shipboard services on that return voyage. He was hospitalized for the entire trip. After a year's rest, he went back to India once more and experienced two more nervous breakdowns.

He tells of sitting in Lucknow, about to address a great crowd of intellectuals, and being overcome by anxiety once again. "I was telling the Lord, 'I can't do it,' when I heard the Lord say to me, 'Stanley, do you want to do this work I have called you to do? You can't because you're full of tension and stress. Turn your life over to me. I will give you all the energy you need.' " E. Stanley Jones did that and went on to serve God powerfully over the next forty years. I spent a week with him in Belleville, Ontario, when he was in his eighties. He was doing thirty-five push-ups every morning. He was fit and in his full powers. The Lord had promised him all the energy he would need to serve him all the days of his life, and he had it.

Whatever illness you're facing right now, your own or that of a loved one, keep in mind that God, not your doctor, has the last word. Through God we have unlimited resources to continue to live abundantly and generously all our remaining days, be they many or few.

13. Facing Financial Fears

One fear that besets many of us is the fear of not having enough, of running out of material resources before life's end. It's not an anxiety confined to the poor. Even the rich are afraid they won't be able to keep what they have and, of course, a lot more are somewhere in the middle, worrying about adequate pension plans and insurance policies and manageable mortgages.

My own theory is that those who have never experienced poverty are more frightened of it than those who have been there. Those who weathered the Depression years of the thirties wouldn't go back to that by choice, but I suspect a lot of us would say that it had its positive aspects. We felt a kinship with our neighbors. We cared for each other. How we love telling our children sad stories of deprivation in those harrowing days. There seems to have been something almost noble about them.

A letter from a parishioner reinforces that theory. He writes, "There is very little which I fear, not that I am a fearless individual, but rather, having lost most of what I have had, what else is to be lost which has value?" This man suggests that his experience helped him reassess what was and was not valuable. Thomas Burton in *Assent to Truth* claims that we surround our lives with much that distracts us from the real purpose of living. Caring for and protecting those distractions causes its own kind of fear and panic.

Our fear of poverty is rooted in our basic attitude toward money. We may feel it's perfectly legitimate to devote our lives to making money, and lots of it. In an earlier chapter, we spoke of the health-and-wealth gospel. It's a seductive message. "You belong to a God who owns all things and he wants you to have it all." God does want to bless us and we need to claim those blessings, but basically that message is heresy. Christ did not die for our sins to make us rich or even healthy. He died to reconcile the world unto himself.

I stumbled into a strange meeting in a hotel in downtown Seattle about a year and a half ago. Several thousand people were gathered, and at the front of the room a group of cheerleaders, in purple and silver garb, were waving pompoms and shouting things like, "Go, unite, fight. You can do it." Several in the crowd came forward to witness to the fact that chanting has been a means of getting them everything they wanted. One man claimed he had chanted an hour a day for three months for a white BMW, and received one. Others had chanted successfully for lower car insurance rates or a better and cheaper apartment. I discovered that these people belonged to a Buddhist sect. That seems incongruous. The Buddhist religion, as you may know, is one which seeks enlightenment rather than salvation. Avarice is considered to be at the heart of human misery. Nevertheless, there are presently half a million people in this particular sect, worldwide, and they are using the chanting of Buddhism in the hope of acquiring material rewards.

There is, as we said, a thread of truth in the health-and-wealth gospel. Jesus promised certain rewards to his disciples: "Truly I say to you, there is no one who has left house or brothers or sisters or mother or father or children or lands for my sake and for the gospel, who will not receive a hundred fold now, in this time, houses and brothers and sisters and children and lands, with persecution and, in the age to come eternal life" (Mark 10:29, RSV). It's a wonderful promise, but we dare not leave out that stipulation, "for my sake and for the gospel". God *is* a generous God who has promised to care for those who have given up all material rewards for the sake of his Kingdom. But, however much or little we own, we are not to make our possessions the focus of our lives and certainly not of our faith.

Henri Nouwen, Roman Catholic priest and Yale professor, has had his diaries published. In them, he tells about returning to Holland to visit his family. At one place, he says poignantly, "I know every word in the language, but do I have a language to say what I truly want to say? . . . I felt lonely, especially because I couldn't share God's gifts with those who are closest to me." But he goes on to make this point in regard to his native land: "Holland feels very self-satisfied, stuffed, busy. There is not much space left to be with God and God alone. Dutch folks are just very busy eating, drinking and going places. They have become a distracted people, a very good, kind and good-natured people, but caught up in too much of everything." The national disease Nouwen comments on is certainly not confined to the Netherlands.

Jesus tells the parable of the rich fool, so worried about having enough that he sets to building bigger barns. We could translate that concern today into amassing larger bank accounts, more insurance, bigger pension plans. In the parable, the rich man is called a fool. "Tonight your soul is required of you (Luke 12:20, RSV). In another story from the gospels, Jesus is confronted by a man who asks him to make his brother divide their inheritance with him. He is certain Jesus will perceive that he is being cheated by his brother and do something about it. By way of reply, Jesus is almost rude. "Who made me a judge or divider over you?" (Luke 12:14, RSV). is his response. Jesus did not come to make sure we got our fair share of property or anything else. He came to proclaim God's Kingdom and offer us the chance to live in that Kingdom, rich or poor.

Nevertheless, there are sincere Christians who are convinced poverty is the only way in the life of faith. Money is evil. Rich people are bad and poor people are good. Actually, money in itself is amoral. Your attitude toward it and use of it are the crucial factors for the Christian. Gert Behanna, author of *The Late Liz,* experienced both wealth and poverty. After a lifetime of too much of everything— too many husbands, too much money, too much booze and drugs, she got converted. One of her first acts as a Christian was to give all her money away. "Who needs it?" she reasoned. "I have God now and he'll take care of me." That was a decision she was to regret. In later years, she wished fervently that she had some of that money to invest in all sorts of Kingdom projects to bless other people in need. She learned too late that poverty was not the only option for a Christian.

Some of us have played at poverty, made a sort of game of it, usually as students. When I was seventeen, I spent a summer in Mexico. I had enlisted in the army and was waiting to be called into service. I withdrew my life's savings, an impressive three hundred dollars earned from any number of summer jobs, and headed south. I went by train from Chicago to Laredo, by bus to Mexico City, enrolled in the University of Mexico, and paid my tuition in advance. I lived for the next three months with a Mexican family, paying room and board. When I finally got back home, again by train and bus, I walked in the front door of our Evanston house with just five cents in my pocket. It was a challenge to make those three hundred dollars stretch that far for that long. But that wasn't poverty. There are youngsters backpacking all over the world these days playing that game. Most of them need only to call home to get out of any real financial crunch.

There are missionary movements that send out men and women with no guarantee of support. One of the largest is run by a friend of many decades. His organization has sent out a thousand missionaries at a time all over the world with no guaranteed salary. I once called him to task for that. "Listen, so many of these people end up in some foreign field, sick and broke and hungry, and missionaries from the mainline denominations end up taking care of them." He just grinned. "You see, Bruce? God does take care of them." I can't argue with that, but I still don't see that as a responsible kind of policy.

The theory is often advanced that the poor are poor and stay poor because they are inherently different than the rest of us—lazy, imprudent, unmotivated, whatever. One theory is that the poor need instant gratification. Their paycheck is spent as soon as it's received. The rich, on the other hand, save some of their resources for the future. An experiment was conducted a while ago to try to prove that point, using rats as usual. There were two groups: fat, pampered rats and lean, hungry rats. Each rat was placed in a pen with two levers. The first lever released one food pellet immediately. The second lever released three pellets, but only after a twelve-second interval. Contrary to expectations, the undernourished rats did the wise thing and learned quickly to delay gratification and to push the lever that produced three pellets. The fat rats invariably pushed the lever delivering instant gratification. Further, when the scrawny rats became well-nourished, they punched the instant gratification lever as well. I'm not sure studies on rats can be applied neatly to human behavior, but the usual rationale for the gap between rich and poor needs to be reexamined.

Two decades ago an American president, Lyndon Johnson, announced with much fanfare a nationwide war against poverty. It is all too obvious that that war was never won, especially in the cities, where streets are strewn with panhandlers, bag ladies, and the homeless. That war is one to which every Christian is committed. If God has blessed us with resources, we are not to despise them, but to use them as the means of helping our desperate brothers and sisters.

On the other hand, we can be far too focused on getting and having, earning and spending. Jesus speaks to us as he did to his disciples in Galilee. "Fear not little flock, for it is your Father's good pleasure to give you the Kingdom" (Luke 12:32, RSV). As members of this Kingdom, we put our trust in the King. We are not to worry about money, portfolios, annuities, or the stock market. That means we can pursue a chosen vocation, whether or not it pays well. A life spent at a job you hate just because it provides great monetary rewards is a tragic life. Again, there is nothing intrinsically wrong with making money. The challenge is to follow God's leading, whatever that means, plenty or want.

If your aim is to amass a fortune for your adult children, I urge you to reconsider that goal. If they succeed financially, let them have the satisfaction of knowing they did it all on their own. In the meantime, invest your money before you die in causes you care about and believe in. Remember, there is no U-haul behind a hearse. In his diary, Jim Elliott, that martyred missionary to South America, said, "He is no fool who gives up that which he cannot keep in order to gain that which he cannot lose."

I read a wonderful story recently about Ignacy Paderewski, the incomparable pianist. Years ago he was asked by two Stanford students to come to the campus and give a concert. He agreed to do so for a fee of $2000. After the concert, the two students showed up backstage looking crestfallen. "Mr. Paderewski, we're terribly sorry," they explained. "We only raised $1600. We will be glad to give you an IOU for the other $400." To their astonishment, Paderewski tore up the $1600 check. "I'm sorry you didn't make it, boys," he said. "I'll tell you what. Pay your expenses with this money, take ten percent of the profit for yourselves, and send me whatever is left."

In later years Paderewski returned to Poland. World War I broke out, and in its aftermath, all of Europe was in desperate straits. Paderewski was about to intervene with the United States to assist his starving countrymen when the decision was made to open our storehouses and ship food to Poland and the rest of Europe. Paderewski made a trip to America to personally thank President Herbert Hoover for the aid. To his amazement, Hoover told him he had been one of those two students at Stanford whose debt the great pianist had magnanimously forgiven, so long before.

It's a heartwarming story, but it ought not to mislead us about Christian stewardship. We do not give with the idea of reciprocity. Christian stewardship is based on trusting the Lord for our future, living in his Kingdom and claiming his promises. You may be intrigued by that Buddhist sect, who hope to chant their way into wealth, but God has something better for his sons and daughters. It's not important how much we have, but whose we are. We belong to an unlimited supplier who promises that, rich or poor, we will always have enough.

14. Facing Hopelessness

A bumper sticker I saw recently offered this advice: "Eat dessert first. Life is uncertain." The author of that one could be suffering from terminal hopelessness, one of the deadliest of diseases. Paul in his New Testament letter to the Corinthians tells us the three greatest things in the world are faith, hope, and love. It follows that the absence of any one of those three has to represent a serious deficiency, particularly for Christians. Hopelessness produces fear, which produces a host of other problems, even illness and death.

Christian hope, unlike most other kinds of hope, is not mere optimism. It's not even a matter of thinking positively: "Cheer up. Things will work out." Christian hope is applied faith. If god himself is here with us in his Holy Spirit, then all things are possible. When we react to the difficult circumstances in life saying, "What's the use? It's all over," we invite spiritual death.

Physicians are telling us that hope, or the lack of it, is the crucial factor in dealing with serious illness. We have already explored this connection between fear and illness. A doctor makes the dread pronouncement, "Well, old friend, you've got cancer," and predicts life expectancy at just a year or two. Any number of patients are gone in just a few months. The diagnosis alone lowered the window-shades of the soul. The inner spark of life seems gone, and death comes prematurely as a result of fear and hopelessness as much as or more than from the actual disease.

Hope and its absence affect that hardnosed world of business. A friend who was for many years a master merchandiser in my city said, "We discovered over the years that when you plan for loss, you get loss. When you plan for profit, you get profit." Fortunately, that man is on our church's ruling body, and he keeps us in that same positive frame of mind. "Let's not plan for a deficit," is his motto.

We lose hope in other people, and that's an especially bitter kind of hopelessness. You bet on a particular person to love you forever, and that person has left, walked out, asked for a divorce. You have no control over that, and the powerlessness that results is a greased slide into a well of hopelessness. Or we lose hope in our own abilities. We bet on ourselves to be always adequate or well or smart or moral, and we fail. We could say that our hope was never solidly based in the first place. There had better be something outside of our own strength and goodness on which to focus our hope.

George Bernard Shaw, that brilliant skeptic, wrote these telling words at the end of his life: "The science to which I pinned my faith is bankrupt. Its counsels, which should have established the millenium, led instead directly to the suicide of Europe. I believed them once. In their name, I helped to destroy the faith of millions of worshippers in the temples of a thousand creeds. And now they look at me and witness the tragedy of an atheist who has lost his faith." I can't mourn the loss of Mr. Shaw's faith in atheism. I just wish he had placed it in the God revealed in the Old and New Testaments, whose Kingdom is eternal.

Christian hope is a hope based on the fact that God is, that he loves us, that he came in Jesus Christ to identify with us. He is present in your life and mine. If you begin with the sure hope of the incarnation, the atonement, the resurrection, and the reality of the indwelling of the Spirit, there is no hopeless situation.

The theme of hope permeates the Old Testament narrative. Joseph, Jacob's favorite son, is sold into slavery by his jealous brothers. Before the timely arrival of the slave traders, he has been put in a well to die. As a slave in Egypt, he finds favor with his master and is put in charge of the household, only to be betrayed again, this time by the lecherous wife of his employer. Imprisoned under false accusations, he interprets a dream for Pharaoh's chief butler, a fellow prisoner, who promises to remember him to the Pharaoh and get him released. Two whole years go by before that comes to pass. Yet Joseph, never daunted, never bitter, is a model of authentic hope. Reunited years later with his treacherous brothers, he is magnanimous. "God meant it for good," he tells them.

Nothing looks more hopeless for the Israelites than their escape from the Egyptians. They are smack up against the Red Sea. The choice seems to be death by drowning or annihilation at the hands of the Egyptian army. But God cares, and God acts. With the miraculous parting of the waters, the Jews are spared and their enemies destroyed.

After forty years of wandering, the promised land is finally taken by the Israelites, but only on the second attempt. The first generation is convinced it is impossible: the enemy too strong, their own forces inadequate. The succeeding generation, though just as aware of the superior force of the enemy, believes God will bless their efforts, and they succeed.

In the 1970s, one of our president's closest advisors was convicted of malfeasance and put in prison. Charles Colson could have been overcome with hopelessness. Instead, God gave him a vision for revamping the prison system. His own experience led him to begin a prison ministry which has brought new hope to prisoners all over our nation, and, indeed, all over the world.

I read a while back about a man named Harry who was faced with a hopeless situation. Harry underwent surgery to have a cancerous bladder removed. Afterward, in the recovery room, his doctor had bad news. His bladder had not been removed. Harry was beyond surgery and even beyond chemotherapy. There was no hope at all. He could expect death almost any moment.

At home, Harry could neither eat nor sleep. He continued to deteriorate, until one morning a letter arrived from a distant relative. At the very bottom she wrote, "Harry, we're praying for you. 'With God all things are possible' " (Matt. 19:26, RSV). Harry, a nonbeliever, immediately checked the verse in an old, never-used Bible. He was stung by the verse and continued to read the New Testament narrative about Jesus, the carpenter of Nazareth.

Oddly enough, he suddenly felt hungry. He called out to his wife that he'd like something to eat. She suggested tea and toast, which would have represented a substantial meal at that point, since he was living on ginger ale. When he protested that he wanted something more, his wife jokingly suggested that he might like a submarine sandwich. That was exactly what he wanted. This man, who had lost fifty pounds, ate a whole sandwich stuffed with salami and peppers and dripping in oil and vinegar. That was just the beginning of the turnaround. He began to pray day and night. He continued to eat. He started chemotherapy and he got well. He is presently an aggressive witness to the fact that God can do all things.

There is an ever-recurring temptation to hopelessness for all of us, and it is helpful to see how Jesus deals with the problem. In one incident, he is confronted by a father whose twelve-year-old daughter is seriously ill. Jairus is a desperate man looking for new solutions. The doctors have done all they can. He has heard of this unusual prophet with power to heal, and it is worth a try. I commend that approach to anyone who is desperately ill and for whom the doctors have done all they can. That desire to try every avenue is motivated by hope and a continued commitment to life.

Jairus is driven by love for his daughter. She is too sick to go anywhere, so he acts for her. His faith is a vicarious faith. He is like those four men who lowered their sick friend through the roof to seek healing from Jesus. Jesus, we read, was moved by *their* faith, and said to the paralytic, "Rise, take up your bed and go home" (Luke 5:24, RSV). In the same way, your faith, your hope, and your prayers can affect the lives of sick and hurting friends.

As Jesus moves to leave with this distraught father, the crowd follows them. In that throng is a woman with a problem no doctor has been able to cure. Mark describes it as an issue of blood. She believes that just touching Jesus' garment will be enough to heal her, and it is. But she is not allowed to slip away unnoticed. Jesus immediately perceives not only that someone has touched him, but that, in Mark's words, "power had gone out of Him." The woman, in fear and trembling, confesses it is she and is told, "Your faith has made you well" (Mark 5:34, RSV).

In just a few short paragraphs, we find Jesus being interrupted twice: first as he is teaching a great crowd beside the sea, and next on the way to minister to a sick little girl. To digress for a bit, Jesus has a good deal to teach us about handling interruptions. Too often I am in a panic over them. I've got an intense schedule, and I don't take kindly to being deflected from it. I'd like to think I'm improving in that department. If the Holy Spirit lives in us, we ought to be an inexhaustible resource. I am coming to see that out of the riches Christ gives us, we have something to give to anyone who asks, whether the timing seems appropriate or not.

While Jesus is still speaking to the woman, messengers arrive with bad news for the father. "Your daughter is dead. Why trouble the teacher any further?" The text indicates that Jesus ignores them. He doesn't argue or try to convince them they are wrong. We need to do the same with skeptics who tell us the situation is hopeless. Ignore them. In this case, Jesus says to Jairus, the ruler of the synagogue, "Do not fear. Only believe" (Mark 5:36, RSV). He says that to us in those crucial times of our lives.

At the house of Jairus at last, Jesus speaks the word of faith even before he sees the little girl. He tells those gathered that the child is not dead, but sleeping. Jesus rebukes the mourners, and they laugh at him. Next, he insures a climate of faith. He puts the doubters, the laughters, the scoffers, out and brings in Peter, James, and John, and the two parents, just those five. When you are faced with a hopeless situation, I advise you to do the same. Perform a doubt-ectomy. Surround yourself, not with skeptics, but with believers. The happy ending is insured with Jesus' words, *"Talitha cumi,"* which mean "Little girl, I say to you, arise." She does so, and then Jesus speaks a further word, instructions to give her something to eat. How eminently practical and earthly. The Lord of the universe is concerned with the physical dimensions of her recovery as much as with its spiritual dimensions.

How do we apply these tactics of Jesus to our own hopeless situations? First, we need to challenge the skeptics, those folks who come around predicting doom and gloom. Don't give in to their pessimism. Doubt the doubters.

Secondly, change your environment. Surround yourself with people who believe all things are possible with God and who will pray that way. That's why worship is so important. In our everyday lives out in the world, all of us are surrounded by cynics and skeptics. A sanctuary filled with believers, called by God to bring hope to hopeless situations, is the climate in which our faith can make us well.

Finally, expect a miracle. Expect something good to happen, even though you are aware it may not. Hope is not a means of manipulating God. It is believing anything is possible and that, whether or not our desperate situation does change, change is possible. We live in hope. Don't let hopelessness keep you from dreaming great dreams and acting out those dreams.

We hold public healing services in our church every two months. I got a moving letter after a recent one. The writer says,

The healing session at UPC has changed my life. I harbored a lot of bitterness and anger toward my father and a relationship with an old boy friend that I had thought I had been over. . . . As I sat in the back pew, I really began to see what bitterness, anger had done to my body. You and some elders were praying with many people. When I walked up . . . the lady [an elder] who was with you looked at me and said, "Jane [not her actual name], God is very pleased with you." I think for the first time in my life I believed it. I was having a lot of back pain that particular morning. After I was prayed for, I still had it. I was disappointed, of course. And I guess I thought I wasn't supposed to be healed. The next morning I was up, and all my pain was gone. Praise the Lord. You know, you always talk about God's dream for us. I think I've always believed it sounded so good, but if only, if only. . . . We can't keep blaming our past, other people, our bodies, for who we are. I feel blessed that at 25 I am catching a grasp of that dream.

In a climate of faith, this young woman found new hope. She is healed of far more than back pain. God has good gifts for us, and one of them is the gift of hope. With it, there are no hopeless situations and no hopeless people. All things are possible.

15. Facing the Unpredictable

For most of us, occurrences that seem out of sync and out of context with all that's gone before are likely to provoke fear. That's natural. We are so made by God that routine makes us comfortable. If you've ever read a bedtime book to a child or grandchild, you know that they usually want to hear the same story over and over again. I sometimes change a word with my little grandson, just for fun, something like: "Red Riding Hood met up with a big, bad bear." He protests vehemently, "No, no! It was a wolf." He knows the story by heart and won't countenance any changes, because the familiar plot is so important.

We love the kind of stories in which we know who the villain is, who the hero is, and when to cheer or boo. That's why old-fashioned melodrama was so popular. We are accustomed to the scenario. The heroine repeats: she can't pay the rent. The villain responds: she must pay the rent. At last the hero appears: he'll pay the rent. "My hero!" she cries. We know what's coming and we love it, even as adults.

We are uncomfortable with those people in the public eye who cannot be put neatly into a good or bad category. We want our heroes to be heroes and our villains to be villains. We want security in our lives. We want guaranteed jobs, guaranteed wages, guaranteed profits, and guaranteed pension plans. We even want a predictable marriage, but let me tell you something, if you haven't already discovered it. You need some spice, some departure from the expected, to survive in marriage.

A young parishioner saved for a whole year in order to take his wife to Hawaii on a birthday trip. He kept his plans secret until her birthday came and over dinner he produced the tickets and hotel reservations. She had always wanted to go and was, of course, thrilled; but her first question was, "What about the kids?" "I've already arranged for a sitter," he said. Every married man or woman can learn from that story. Build in some serendipities. Don't settle into those too-comfortable ruts.

A. G. Buckham says, "Monotony is the awful reward of the careful." Even success can be boring. At a Christian conference a while back, I met an old friend, an astute businessman whose other vocation involves leadership in a citywide ministry. We visited for an hour or so, and among other things, he confessed to feeling burned out in his job. He had inherited the family business, and it had doubled in size every year for almost ten years. There are now offices in twenty-seven foreign countries. After an hour of so, I said, "Friend, you're not burned out. You are bored. You've done it all, and you need new challenges." He brightened immediately. "Maybe you're right," he said. "Maybe I need to find something new to do." His success had settled into dull routine.

The French writer Jean Anouilh says, "Some people like to make a little garden out of life and walk down a path." It sounds idyllic, doesn't it? But most gardens have borders which are clearly circumscribed. Within that area, you plant seeds and tend weeds and are careful to confine your walking to the path. Life is stripped of any challenge or mystery. We need more stimulation than that.

I overheard two women discussing the situation of a friend trapped in an apparently unrewarding marriage.

"Why does she stay with him?" asked one. Her companion had the answer. "She never knows what will happen next."

Dr. John Rowe, associate professor of medicine at Harvard, has come up with a thumbnail sketch of the man least likely to suffer a heart attack: Among other things, he is someone lacking physical or mental alertness, without drive, without ambition, without competitive spirit, who has never had a deadline in his life. He has a poor appetite and, in addition to his low blood pressure, blood sugar, uric acid and cholesterol, he has a low income. That may describe the safe way to live, but it is a life so unexciting that a heart attack might look like a welcome escape.

The danger in this desire for the routine and the comfortable is that within that framework, we tend to think we are in control. We have made the point earlier that this insistence on control is one of the most apt descriptions of sin. Particular sins vary greatly, from the socially acceptable to those for which we put people in jail. But the source of most of those sins is the desire to control your life, the lives of your family and friends, and even God. Denis Diderot, French encyclopedist, says, "Watch out for the fellow who talks about putting things in order. Putting things in order always means getting other people under control." In its purest form, that is what sin is all about, whether you are a mobster or simply a manipulative parent who looks so pure and self-sacrificing in the world's eyes.

Unfortunately, our efforts to control don't cease at the door of the sanctuary. Even Sunday morning worship services tend to fall into all-too-predictable patterns. The first year in my present parish, I preached a sermon called "Voices from the Balcony." Some students were planted around the balcony section of the sanctuary, and, assuming the roles of various Old and New Testament characters, they shouted out at intervals, interrupting the sermon. The congregation, unprepared for this outburst, reacted strongly. Some said, "I'll never forget *that* sermon. God really got my attention." A few were offended. "Don't ever do that again. It absolutely spoiled the solemnity of worship for me." Even in worship, we have a need to feel in control. That's why the bulletin has assumed such importance. We want to know exactly what's coming and in what order for the next hour. Worship is the last place where we would welcome the unpredictable, even if it is a spontaneous movement of the Holy Spirit.

Many of Jesus' movements in his three-year ministry appear to be somewhat unpredictable to his followers, perhaps especially the jumble of events during that last week in Jerusalem before the crucifixion. The disciples warn against going there at all. His opponents will be waiting to trap him. It is not a safe place. Nevertheless, Jesus insists they celebrate the Passover there. Unpredictable.

His entry by means of an impromptu parade is once again a strange twist of plot. Let's consider the details. In the middle of all of the turmoil of a city crammed with visitors preparing for Passover, Jesus suddenly announces that someone should fetch a donkey. It is very likely one they have seen previously, perhaps even one belonging to a friend. You wonder how the disciples react to this plan for a parade. A few, the more adventurous, might welcome it. "Just what we need—a change of pace."

I think many more would have an anxiety attack. "Oh no. Does the Master know what he's doing? Does he understand the danger? Does he realize the temple authorities are out to kill him, and us as well?"

I like to speculate on how a contemporary church body might have reacted to the idea of that hastily assembled parade. We can hear the objections. Has the long-range planning committee been told about this? Has stewardship okayed the funds for the donkey? Has the administration department considered the insurance needs, applied for a permit? Has the official board (in Jesus' case Peter, James, and John) given its approval? This Palm Sunday parade is a strange one, no question about it. It is also a puny one, by today's standards; a one-float parade. One man on a donkey is the extent of it.

On the surface, that Palm Sunday parade looks utterly spur-of-the-moment, but we have come to see that Jesus is far from capricious. Zechariah had predicted that the Messiah would arrive in just such a way. "Fear not, daughter of Zion. Behold your king is coming, sitting on an ass's colt" (Zech. 9:9, RSV). The Messiah's coming in that triumphal entry on that first Palm Sunday evokes a number of strange responses: short-lived adulation from the crowd, implacable opposition from the Pharisees, and vascillating obedience from many of the disciples.

It occurs to me that as Christians you and I are *s*ervants *o*f an *u*npredictable *L*ord. In other words, SOUL sisters and brothers. We can't chart out how God will intervene in our lives or what joys and misadventures lie ahead. That's why we need to give up our expectations of what life is going to be like, and expect him to surprise us. God loves us too much to let us suffer from boredom.

Last fall I read this item in the personal column of our local paper: "To the person who administered CPR late on the morning of 11/25 to Marcelino Q. downtown Seattle, First and Pike. We are very grateful to you for saving our father's life. You have given us something to be thankful for on this Thanksgiving." Somebody passing by, on the way to work, to school, to a pressing errand, saw someone in need and stopped in the manner of the famous Good Samaritan. I don't know that person, but I'm making him an honorary soul brother.

A friend in middle life went with her church on a mission to Haiti and found that God had some totally unexpected experiences for her. She writes:

Haiti was a time of tremendous personal growth for me. In the poverty of the poorest of the poor, I was made the richest of the rich. . . . All a gift to me from the beautiful, suffering people of Haiti. . . . Hands—I never knew what they were for, as long as they were covered with rings and lotions. Now for the first time, I see my hands as being gifts from God because they have been used to heal, to soothe, to bind up ulcerated feet with the skin ripped off and toes hanging on by strands of ligament and muscles. Thank God for hands and thank God for arms and thank God for lips and eyes, all of which speak one word so sweetly, and that word is "love."

That Palm Sunday parade we have been discussing, however unpredictable, served God's ends in a multitude of ways and set the stage for all of the events to follow, both tragic and triumphant. Martin Bell, in his book *The Way of the Wolf,* writes movingly about another parade, God's eternal parade.

"I think God must be very old and very tired. Maybe He used to look splendid and fine in His general's uniform, but no more. He's been on the march a long time, you know. And look at his rag tag little army. All He has for soldiers are you and me—dumb little army. Listen! The drumbeat isn't even regular. Everyone is out of step. . . . He may be old, and He may be tired, but He knows where He's going and He means to take every last one of His tiny soldiers with Him, only there aren't going to be any forced marches. . . . Most of us are afraid and lonely and would like to hold hands or cry or run away, and we don't know where we are going, and we can't seem to trust God, especially when it's dark out and we can't see Him. But He won't go on without us. And maybe that's why it's taking so long.

If you are facing the unpredictable right now in your life, I suggest you look for God's gift to you in it. The uninterrupted routine of work, eat, sleep, play—however pleasant—is not enough for any of us. It is those new, unexpected challenges that force us to depend upon the resources of God and to find the inner strength he gives. That march of eternity that Martin Bell writes so movingly about is life's greatest adventure.

16. Facing Rejection

One of the low points of my life last year occurred the week before Christmas, when I conducted a funeral for a nineteen-year-old suicide. I did not know the young man, except through his grandparents, but he was apparently a youngster full of gifts and promise. He took his life when the girl he was in love with rejected him. I think I have some understanding of his state of mind.

I was sitting in a foxhole in the Vosges mountains in the dead of winter, cold, wet, and hungry. We had spent four days there, looking down across the valley at the enemy. I thought things couldn't get worse, but they did. When our supply group caught up to us with hot meals and the mail, I had a letter from my long-term high school sweetheart. It was one of those famous "Dear John" letters, except it began "Dear Bruce." She went on to say she had found somebody else. At any age, from nineteen to eighty and probably beyond, rejection from the one you love is the cause of enormous pain.

Psychologists tell us that the most primal and basic fear for all of us is the fear of abandonment. At some level, we still remember those early weeks and months when we cried for food or love or a dry diaper, wondering if anybody would ever come. Those feelings don't go away. All of us—overachievers, underachievers, or moderate achievers—still experience that fear of abandonment.

It's not surprising, then, that the God revealed through the patriarchs and prophets and, supremely, through his Son, Jesus Christ, is portrayed as someone who understands rejection. Speaking through the prophets and the psalmist, we hear him say over and over again, "I have loved you as a husband loves a bride, and yet you have rejected me." His love is vulnerable, in that we have the power to accept or reject it. The prophets described the Messiah to come as a man despised, rejected of men, and that was an accurate prediction. Throughout his arrest, trial, and execution at Golgotha, Jesus experienced ultimate rejection.

The fear of rejection is endemic to the human race. In his autobiography *The Moon's a Balloon,* David Niven writes about his version of this particular fear. He calls it the imposter syndrome. All his life he expected some little man to turn up and pat him on the back and tell him to get off the set, the jig is up, that he's been found out as a no-talent man posing as a great actor. Some of the most prominent people in business have similar feelings. "What if the stockholders or employees discover how little I know? I feel like an imposter in this chief executive role. I don't deserve to be here."

Dick Halverson, Presbyterian minister and chaplain of the United States Senate, is one of the founders of the presidential prayer breakfasts where heads of state and VIPs from all over the world gather. Here is what he says about his fears: "In some ways I'm a very private person. I've always struggled with low self-image. Because of that image, I'm easily intimidated. To this day, if I have to walk into a room full of strangers, I must brace myself for the experience. Although I think I have accepted my low self-image, I compensate for it with a gregarious air."* It seems that low self-esteem and fear of rejection have little to do with our status or accomplishments.

*From an interview with Richard Myer, *Faith at Work,* September 1987.

In my own life, I have been through a dark time of feeling rejected. A stutter and stammer that I had overcome in teenage years returned. I dreaded answering the telephone, fearful I would be unable to speak clearly. My fear of rejection during that period was not entirely the result of paranoia. I was in an organization where a bitter power struggle was being waged, with my own position eroding almost daily. A story I read at the time about Fiorella La-Guardia, onetime mayor of New York and known as "The Little Flower," prompted in me a special empathy. He was hospitalized with a severe intestinal problem when a message from his colleagues arrived: "The City Council wishes you a quick recovery by a vote of nineteen to twelve."

Each of us develops a strategy for coping with this built-in fear of rejection. One obvious one is withdrawal or shyness. We seek safety in going unnoticed. We reach out to no one lest we be rebuffed. Jesus commanded the disciples to "love one another as I have loved you" (John 15:12, RSV). Shyness utterly stifles the ability to do that and, in that sense, could be considered a sin. You retreat from any attempt to love or be loved. Shyness can have other long-term consequences. James Lynch, medical researcher for Johns Hopkins, in his book *The Broken Heart,* claims loneliness is the number one medical killer.

Perhaps your coping strategy is to be a people-pleaser, the very reverse of shyness. The rationale is that if you can become everything I want you to be, I will surely love you. Don't count on it. In the last analysis, everybody's friend is nobody's friend, and our own self-seeking is all too apparent. People-pleasing is a terrible tyranny.

We can cope by a third strategy—outrageous behavior. Our unspoken message is, "Who cares?" Of course we care, but acting as if we don't forestalls rejection. You may, on the other hand, cope by becoming the rejector. These are life's critics, professional and amateur, people who pronounce judgment on everyone and everything. They are the arbiters of taste and behavior, measuring all against their own impeccable standards.

A book came out several years ago featuring some of the most scathing reviews published over the centuries by a number of professional critics. My favorite is this Voltaire review from 1768: "It is a vulgar and barbarous drama, which would not be tolerated by the vilest populace in France or Italy. One would imagine this piece to be the work of a drunken savage." He was talking about Shakespeare's *Hamlet*. There are a lot of people who see themselves as professional critics—even without recompense. They find the flaw in everything, which is a protective device and one way to say, "Before you reject me, I will reject you."

A man with this sort of strategy wrote recently: "I am afraid you will reject me, therefore I withold myself to protect myself. . . . You do reject me, but I do it first. . . . Then project my rejection on you. You merely do what I set you up to do in order to protect myself." We all know people like that. They defy us to like them.

The powerful and wealthy have a built-in system to overcome this basic fear. They can live behind high walls with electric gates and gatekeepers. They can hire a battery of secretaries who will keep the world from intruding. A man named David Miller went on trial in Pittsburgh for embezzling 1.3 million dollars from six companies over a twenty-year period. In his trial, a psychiatrist was called as a witness for the defense. He proposed Mr. Miller should be excused because he had a compulsory need to buy love and friendship. So do a good many of us, and enough money or power or position can lead us to believe that we have succeeded.

Professional people can have the edge in hiding this fear of rejection. Doctors, lawyers, judges, pastors can pose behind a professional mask. The professional personage is a substitute for the person who may get hurt or rejected. Perhaps the most salient fear of rejection is the one operating in dating. We are so afraid of being rejected if we openly give ourselves in love or friendship or marriage.

I believe a point system is actually at work on some subconscious level in this search for a satisfying relationship. This is how it works: Young is better than old. If I'm young I get a point. Beautiful and handsome is better than plain, so the beautiful and handsome get another point. Wealthy is better than poor and gives you an additional point. A status job or profession is the source of yet another point. We can walk into a singles bar or any place where there are datable people and start looking for someone with a similar point rating. Somebody with more points than I is an unpromising candidate for my attentions. Those with less are unworthy of them. People have an uncanny way or sorting themselves out, the goal being to avoid rejection.

The fear of rejection is rooted primarily in self-centeredness. I think I am the center of the universe, and all the rest of the people in the room are moving around me and wondering how I'm doing. I walk into a room, concerned about being dressed right, about looking cool and sophisticated. I see myself as the center of the party and naturally I am self-conscious. The truth is nobody cares. They're all busy worrying about the impression they're making. They don't even know I'm there.

At the heart of our fear of rejection is a sense of worthlessness—no self-esteem. Most of us suffer from this part of the time. We need to be reminded that whatever we think of ourselves, Jesus Christ loves and esteems us. He died for us. By our invitation, his Spirit lives in us. We have supreme worth.

Our low self-esteem may be the result of guilt or guilt feelings. Our guilt may be the result of transgressions against brothers and sisters or against God. It may be false guilt, vague feelings that you are not living up to the expectations of Mom or Dad or someone else.

God has a solution for our fear of rejection. We need not be self-conscious in a room full of people. We can be Christ-conscious. Matthew writes, "He who receives you receives me, and he who receives me receives him who sent me" (Matt. 10:40, RSV). If we are his children, we are walking love. We begin to see other people for who they are: insecure and afraid of rejection, just as we were and, at times, still are. No matter how angry or hostile others seem to be, they are people like ourselves, wanting acceptance.

A friend bought a dog last year, a three-year-old malamute and a beautiful animal. The dog had one bad habit. When the family was away, he entertained himself by singing. The next-door neighbor did not find that endearing and called both the police and the humane society to complain. My friend managed to train his dog not to sing, but the situation with the neighbor continued to be strained. At Christmas, my friend made up his mind to call on the neighbor and bring a gift. He packed a box with home-smoked salmon and other goodies. "I went next door," he said, "to bring my present and wish the family a hearty Merry Christmas. My neighbor seemed bewildered. He couldn't believe we still cared about him and wanted to have a relationship."

We all need reassurance that we are esteemed and have worth, and that need can be a more potent motivator than money. A man ran an ad in a Chicago paper for a whole week: "Wanted: housekeeper for motherless home, two small children. Live in. $425 per month." He got no responses. The following week he ran the same ad, except that instead of $425 per month, he wrote, "Name your own salary." He was besieged with replies, and not a single respondent named a figure as high as $425. It was enough, apparently, to feel needed and to be trusted to know your own worth.

That fear of rejection is operating in all of us at some level, and, as we relate to others, we have to find ways to overcome it. One is by loving aggressively, going the second mile. A pastor, William Steiger, tells of being in a group where he was asked about the influential people in his life. He mentioned a teacher who had introduced him to Tennyson and much more thirty years ago. "Have you ever thanked her for that?" he was asked. That was enough to prompt him to write this woman a letter. He didn't even know if she was still alive, or where she lived. He wrote to the school where they had met, and eventually received this reply.

My dear Willie: I can't tell you how much your note meant to me. I am in my eighties, living alone in a small room, cooking my own meals, lonely and like the last leaf of fall lingering behind. You'll be interested to know that I taught school for fifty years, and yours is the first note of appreciation I ever received. It came on a blue, cold morning, and it cheered me as nothing has in many years.

Remember, too, that our own inborn fear of rejection can be a bridge to someone else's life. There is a book out by the psychiatrist Gerald Jampolsky, mentioned earlier on, titled *Love is Letting Go of Fear*. In it he tells of serving in a psychiatric ward in a San Francisco hospital and being called at two o'clock in the morning to deal with an emergency. A severe schizophrenic had gone berserk. He was locked in a room and had torn loose a piece of moulding in which a huge nail was embedded. He was brandishing that weapon wildly, yelling loudly. Two male nurses, both of small stature, urged Dr. Jampolsky to go in. They'd be right behind him. "I was terrified," he said. "I looked through the window and there was this man, 6′4″, 280 pounds, swinging a club. I yelled through the door, 'Hey, in there! This is Dr. Jampolsky. I'm a psychiatrist and I see you in there, and I'm terrified. I'm scared spitless. How about you? Aren't you afraid?' " "You bet I am," was the reply. For the next five or ten minutes they acted as each other's therapists, talking about their fears. After a while, when the patient calmed down, the doctor was able to enter and administer some medication. "We need to learn how to use our own fear of rejection as a bridge to other people's lives," was Dr. Jampolsky's conclusion.

Finally, there is another kind of rejection, one which too few of us know much about. Matthew's gospel quotes Jesus as saying, "Blessed are you when men revile you and persecute you and utter all kinds of evil against you falsely on my account. Rejoice and be glad, for your reward is great in heaven" (Matt. 5:11,12, RSV).

We need to emphasize that the key phrase here is "on my account." There are some pitfalls for Christians in interpreting these verses. We are too quick to think we are rejected because of our message, and refuse to entertain the idea that our own personalities and methods are in themselves unlovely. Secondly, we cannot use this text as a basis for seeking rejection. That would be pointless and masochistic. On the other hand, there is a dichotomy operating

here. We cannot always be loving and accepting and un-
judgmental and still be identified with Christ and his Kingdom. All along the way, we must make choices, and some
of those will be unpopular choices, for which we may very
well be rejected. Those are the times to "Rejoice and be
glad for your reward is great in heaven."

Rejection is and was something our Lord knew about
firsthand, as do we. The fear of it can stunt our emotional
growth and inhibit our relationships. But we have a choice.
We can use it, as Dr. Jampolsky did, as a bridge into someone else's life, and we can begin, with God's help, to love
aggressively and establish an island of security for our simi-
larly fearful, insecure brothers and sisters.

17. Facing the Past

There are some people, I know, who have a hard time making peace with the past because it was glorious and successful. In the light of the past, the present years seem meaningless and unexciting. What happens when you are no longer the chief executive, the football star, the professional person in great demand? That's a special kind of pain that requires reassessing your life and your worth and trusting God with the future. But there are many more of us who fear facing the past because it was unhappy or shameful, a past of which we are far from proud. Those memories haunt us, and we are unable to make peace with them.

Nevertheless, I believe memory is one of God's best gifts to us. James Barrie, the author of *Peter Pan,* wrote, "God gave us our memories so that we might have roses in December." And that's a wonderful concept. When you are depressed, when you can't sleep, when you are old or sick or suffering through difficulties, your memories can trigger images of all the people who have loved you and blessed you. All the bright, beautiful times of your life can be brought out of the storehouse of your memory, and they make the hard times bearable.

On the other hand, Austin O'Malley has said, "Memory is a crazy woman that hoards colored rags and throws away food." Your memory is a bag lady, keeping all sorts of things that have no worth. Yet your memory is who you are. It is your uniqueness. Your very soul is shaped by the stuff you choose to remember. No wonder Paul wrote to the Philippians, "Whatever is true, whatever is honorable, whatever is just, whatever is pure, whatever is lovely, whatever is gracious, if there is any excellence, if there is anything worthy of praise, think about these things" (Phil. 4:8, RSV). He advises us to put genuine treasures in our memory bank.

We have come through a period when some well-known Christian leaders have had the past catch up with them and destroy their ministries, or so it would seem. I sometimes wonder how Jimmy Swaggart felt while his past was largely still secret. Few, if any, knew of his indiscretions. H. L. Mencken once defined self-respect in this way: "It's that secure feeling that no one is as yet suspicious." I think he's wrong. There is no security in that feeling. That is not how God made us. I can't imagine that Jimmy Swaggart felt secure as he stood before a worldwide audience to preach morality, integrity, and fidelity, all the while aware of his own dark sin. I could be wrong, but I bet he experienced all kinds of spasms and pains, a knotted stomach and sweaty palms. I don't think people with a shameful past have any sense of security.

But there are ways of coping with our guilt feelings that most of us are familiar with. One is to act innocent. Psychiatrists call it denial. It is a means of covering up, and it began early on. When God asks Adam about eating the fruit of the tree of knowledge, he says, "Eve made me do it." When Eve is confronted, she says, "The snake made me do it." Cain, the world's first murderer, is asked about his brother and responds with innocence: "Am I my brother's keeper?"

Another ploy is to go on the attack. In Jimmy Swaggart's case, he was one of the first to throw stones at Jim Bakker of the PTL ministry. Our vigorous efforts to root out certain kinds of sin are often a smoke screen for our own unsavory behavior.

A third strategy is to excuse ourselves on the basis of special privilege. "I am doing so much for the Lord, I don't need to follow the rules as other people do. We can con ourselves into thinking we are so instrumental to God's work that we are entitled to mansions and limousines and air-conditioned doghouses.

But the most dangerous strategy of all is to start rewriting the laws. For example: adultery is so common that "we took a congregational vote on the issue and we're changing the law." The Episcopalians of New Jersey have done that. They have publicly condoned sex outside of marriage and the practice of homosexuality, simply because everybody is doing it. They apparently feel the need to keep in step with the times, and my own denomination may be on its way to similar accommodations. Unfortunately, the Christian does not have the option of voting on what's right or wrong. God has laid down the guidelines and called us to follow them. There are absolutes and, yes, they seem archaic by today's standards, but we are called to walk that straight and narrow path.

We speculated on how Jimmy Swaggart felt before disclosure came, but let's bring it closer to home. I am not an adulterer—yet. I say *yet,* because the Bible says, "Let anyone who thinks that he stands take heed lest he fall" (1 Cor. 10:12, RSV). But there are nights when the ghosts of Christmas past creep into my bedroom between two and four in the morning and rattle their chains. I alternately feel shame, fear, and rage, as I contemplate the past; what I have done and what has been done to me, as well as all those stupid choices that I must now and forever live with.

My past, recent or going way back to the beginning of my life, is there to haunt me. I can remember being part of a gang of fourth graders who picked on a second grader, tied him up, and tortured him. I was part of that, and I am aware of the bentness and the brokenness in me. My mind is a computer chip storing everything I have ever done or experienced, good or bad, just and unjust. Nothing is lost.

It's all recorded for playback, whenever you and I plug in. The problem is to somehow make memory our friend instead of our enemy.

There is a footnote to thirteenth-century history that seems apropos. There were many intercity wars at that time in Italy. The Florentines were attacking Sienna with little success. Sienna felt very smug behind its great, thick walls, confident its vast stores of food would last through any siege. The Florentines started building catapults, and the citizens of Sienna watched in horror as they realized what those were to be used for. Dead donkeys were to be hurled into the city in the hope that their decay and demise would touch off the plague. I feel like that with those middle-of-the-night memories. Somebody is catapulting dead donkeys into my life to cause a stink, and their decay will eventually kill me.

Our fears of the past have a double focus. First of all, if we're Christians, we fear God's judgment. If we have broken his law and done it consciously, we can expect retribution, and we should be fearful about that. Secondly, we're afraid of exposure before our peers. Will those past ugly deeds come to light for all to see? A judge in our state understood this fear of exposure. A twenty-two-year-old man who had piled up $337 in traffic fines appeared in his court. When he was unable to pay the fines, the judge had a solution. A jail term would cost the city $30 a day, and that didn't seem fair to the taxpayers. Instead, the offender was ordered to spend seventy-five hours sitting in a folding chair in front of City Hall. His punishment was public humiliation, and, to me, that would be a bigger deterrent than jail.

The Gospels present us with a telling story of a woman whose past has caught up with her, and for whom public exposure took a nasty turn. The woman caught in adultery is brought to the temple courts and Jesus is asked if he does not agree that she should be stoned, according to the law of Moses. The scribes and Pharisees are using this poor, broken woman to serve their own ends. It is another attempt to trap Jesus. If he says, "Don't stone her," he will be breaking the temple law. If he says, "Stone her," he will be breaking Roman law. Only the conquerors have the right to kill. His enemies are sure they had him on this issue.

Instead of replying, Jesus bends down and writes on the ground with his finger. What in the world does he write? We're not told, and that's one of the first questions I'm going to ask when I get to heaven. He might be writing the Ten Commandments in an effort to put the woman's sin in a larger context. He might be naming some of the sins of the accusers, those men both young and old who are so bent on justice. Perhaps he doesn't write anything of significance, just doodles—using that as a stalling tactic to control his rage, rage that God's servants would be so eager for violence and so duplicitous. We know he looks up long enough to say, "If any one of you is without sin, let him be the first to throw a stone at her" (John 8:7, RSV). One by one, beginning with the oldest, they leave. They understand the message. Everyone is redeemable, or no one is.

Jesus then turns his attention to the woman. "Woman, where are they? Has no one condemned you?" "No one, sir," she says. "Neither do I condemn you" (John 8:11, RSV). Notice, he does not say she is forgiven. She has not come in faith or in penitence, as we all must in order to be forgiven. She was caught and dragged there. She does not receive forgiveness, but neither does she receive condemnation. God sent not his Son into the world to condemn the world, or anyone in it, but that we might have life. How-

ever, Jesus cautioned the woman to "go and sin no more."
He was urging her to learn from this experience and to
change her conduct.

In order to face our past with faith, we need to believe
that Jesus does not condemn us. Beyond that, we can claim
forgiveness if we come penitently and in faith and determine to sin no more. Let those shabby deeds come to light.
The adulterous woman was dragged there. I suggest you
turn yourself in. Talk to a brother or sister in the faith, or
your pastor.

If you are to face the past with faith, you need to forgive
yourself, and that's hard. It's hard for me to forgive myself
for the ways in which I have hurt others. It's hard for me
to forgive the dumb decisions that have led to heartache for
myself and the people I love. We can do so only as we
experience God's forgiveness. Let us count ourselves
among those debtors we pray to forgive each time we say
the Lord's Prayer.

Facing the past with faith means forgiving our enemies.
If we really are forgiven for all our misdeeds, we can prove
it by loving and forgiving and acting in the best interest of
others, even those we love or like least in the world. In a
new book about Hollywood called *Anecdotes,* there is a story
about Louis Selznick, one of the early moguls of the film
industry. He was a victim of persecution as a Jew in Russia
and consequently fled to Hollywood, and went on to
become a famous movie producer. In 1917, the revolution
erupted and Czar Nicholas was deposed. Selznick sent him
a cable:

When I was a poor boy in Kiev, some of your policemen were
not kind to me stop I came to America and prospered stop Now

hear with regret you are out of a job stop Feel no ill will stop If you will come to New York can give you a fine position acting in pictures stop Salary no object stop Reply my expense stop.

Now that's a magnanimous kind of forgiveness we could all emulate with those people we like the least. Do something that reflects your own gratitude for forgiveness.

Face the past with no regrets. Let go of the regrets about those stupid things that were done to you or you have done. Let God use all that garbage from the past for compost. As you stay awake nights reliving all the stupid acts and decisions you wish you could change, believe God can use it all to bless you ultimately.

Finally, walk in the light. As we grow in faith and maturity, we ought to sin less and less, but we will sin again. That's our nature. The Apostle John tells us in his New Testament letter, "He is faithful and just and will forgive our sins" (1 John 1:9, RSV). James writes, "Confess your sins one to another, and pray for one another, that you may be healed" (James 5:16, RSV). In other words, don't wait until you are caught, until your sins are exposed by others. Walk in the light.

It comes down to a choice. We can face the past by reliving our sins day by day, grinding our teeth over those who have sinned against us and by regretting all the foolish decisions that we are now forced to live with. Or we can live by grace, the amazing grace John Newton wrote about in his famous hymn.

Newton was born in England about two hundred and fifty years ago, the only child of a devout Christian mother who dedicated him to God at birth. His mother prayed with him and for him every day of his early life and filled his mind with scripture. When he was seven, she died, leaving him in the charge of a worldly, uncaring father. He went to sea at an early age and, in his own words, "I went to Africa that I might be free to sin to my heart's content." He became a slaver, that most despicable of all trades, trafficking in human life. In an odd turn of events, he became a slave himself. He was bought by an African woman under whose table he had to beg for a crust of bread. Eventually, he escaped and got back to sea. He was pumping bilge in the hold during a severe storm, certain the ship was about to sink, when he remembered the Jesus his mother had told him about.

On that day, March 10, 1748, he was converted, and he felt God's call to return to England to preach. The Church of England was in sad shape at the time, in the control of worldly, fox-hunting bishops and unconverted laity. Newton and some of his colleagues became the first generation of clergy to be termed *evangelical.* Historians have since labeled them the second founders of the Church of England. Newton was still preaching at a very advanced age when a friend advised him to take it easy. He said, "What? Shall an old African blasphemer stop while he can still speak at all?" He kept on preaching.

The last recorded story of Newton reveals the single driving force of his life. In a casual meeting with an acquaintance on the street, he confessed, "My memory is nearly gone, but I remember two things: that I am a great sinner, and that I have a great Savior." By that amazing grace Newton wrote about, we too can be forgiven. We can forgive ourselves and our enemies and, putting all regrets aside, begin to walk in the light. It's the only way to face those fears of the past.

18. Facing the Future

The emotionally healthy person lives in the now, and we Christians might even say that eternity is nothing more or less than endless now. But it is also true that our expectations for the future are as much a shaping force in our lives as are our past experiences. The future is that mysterious, distant landscape on which is fastened the shape of our dreams and goals and long-range plans. There are few truly successful men and women who do not have clearly marked-out and written-down personal goals, and then there are those visionaries whose dreams will affect a whole generation and even future generations. Aspirations for the future determine the direction of my life, and the direction of my life determines who I am right now. No wonder it's frightening to face the future.

One frightening dimension of the future is its certainty—the inescapable certainty of our own death and the death of friends or family members. I'm always astonished to hear someone begin a sentence with, "If I die . . ." No one is going to get out of this alive. Every organism goes through a cycle, one which is inevitable. An organism may be made up of one single individual, or it may be a group, such as a family, a church, or a nation. The same cycle prevails. Organisms are born, they grow, they peak, they decline and diminish, and they die.

Someone has called death the great obscenity of our time, in the way that sex was the great unspoken subject of the nineteenth century. Today's men and women, afraid to contemplate death, have relegated the subject to comedians and comedy writers, who make jokes about it. George Burns says, "There is no reason for me to die. I already died in Altoona." Erma Bombeck, planning her gravestone epitaph, suggests, "Big deal! I'm used to dust." Lily Tomlin predicts, "There will be sex after death; we just won't be able to feel it." With more poignancy than humor, Andy Rooney writes, "Death is just a distant rumor to the young." Not so for those of us who have ceased to be young!

Even those professionals who are paid to deal with death and dying in our hospitals tend to discuss death in shorthand, often using acronyms. Acronyms are used in that setting to describe other life problems. Nurses tell me that "LOLINAD" means a little old lady in no apparent distress. But there are any number of euphemisms used in dealing with death. For example, when chemotherapy fails to cure Mrs. Jones's cancer, the professionals offer this explanation, "Mrs. Jones failed chemotherapy."

A friend who is a gifted physician and dedicated Christian took early retirement for reasons that are disquieting. He felt that the obligations of the medical profession required him to do things that were not in line with God's best for his people. People today are so angered at the diminishment of life that they are demanding full health to the very end. Heroic measures are being used to prolong life at any cost. According to my friend, those monies should more appropriately be directed to the young and the poor. I find my own strength and abilities diminishing these days. It is an annoyance, and I resent it, but it is absolutely normal. It certainly beats the alternative.

We fear the future, then, because of its certainty, but we are equally fearful in terms of its uncertainty. We do not know clearly what our life span will be. We have no guarantees on our health, or the health of loved ones, nor can we with any assurance plot the future of our churches, or even our nation. Futurologists tell us that in the human arena, the future is systemic rather than linear. That means that at any point on the graph, there are multiple options and choices. We do not move in a predictable line. We cannot scientifically predict what individuals will do, let alone what strange things, wonderful or disastrous, will happen to alter the course of human events during our own lives.

Ours is a great nation, and most of us feel privileged to live in it. We like to think it will endure forever, but that isn't likely. History reminds us of the rise and fall of the great powers over the centuries. I'm sure every ruler believes his land and his name will go on forever. Shelley captures this in one of his poems, "Ozymandias." He paints a picture of an ancient monument toppled over in a desolate, barren wasteland with only this legend remaining: "My name is Ozymandias, king of kings: look on my works, ye mighty, and despair!"

For reasons we can't explain, national supremacy has continued to move from east to west, the most obvious successions being from Egypt to Greece, to Rome, to France, to Britain, to our own land. No nation seems able to stay on top of the world ant heap for very long. We're already losing some major economic battles to Japan.

John Naisbitt in his milestone book, *Megatrends,* described the changes that would occur at the end of the eighties. Now he is giving prophetic insights about the nineties, this last decade of the twentieth century—among them, that the middle class will become larger and more affluent, that a renaissance in arts and literature will emerge. We will see the decline of the cities and the end of the welfare state. English will become the world's universal language. The electronic media will be globalized and individualized. We will all have cellular phones and talk to whomever we choose at any given moment. He also predicts that the new frontier of opportunity will be the Pacific Rim, which would substantiate the power-moves-west theory.

All of this may very well take place, but then again, it may not. An epidemic of world proportion could wipe out much of the human race, and all these reasoned predictions may be irrelevant.

Our own personal plans also have a good chance of being derailed, but that ought not to limit our dreaming. Dreams are what separate human beings from the animals. Animals have no hopes, no long-range goals. They simply exist to eat, sleep, procreate, and die. But we, made in the image of God, are capable of creativity, of imagining beyond the present, of projecting both good and bad expectations for ourselves and the whole human race.

There are at least three scenarios most of us project into the future which add to our fears. First is that we will die before we reach our goals. That's not a happy prospect. One of the saddest things we pastors do is to bury young people who die long before what seems to be their time.

Then again, we may outlive the successful fulfillment of our dreams. That is a sad experience. To be moved to the sidelines in life watching others take center stage is depressingly sad. Suppose you are a Pete Rose, who must now live with all of that fame and adulation behind him.

But perhaps the saddest scenario is to die unfulfilled, whether you have been a success or a failure. You may live to a ripe old age, full of regrets and unsettling questions. A number of people of faith in the Bible ended their lives on that note. They did not see in their lifetime what God had promised them.

We are surprised to read of some of the people who put themselves in that category. Hugo Grotius, the father of modern international law, said at the end of his life, "I have accomplished nothing worthwhile in my life." John Quincy Adams, sixth president of the United States, wrote in his diary, "My life has been spent in vain and idle aspirations, and in ceaseless rejected prayers that something would be the result of my existence beneficial to my species." Even the brilliant writer Robert Louis Stevenson wrote for his own epitaph, "Here lies one who meant well, tried a little and failed much."

Facing the future seems to be a catch-22. If we don't dream, we cease to be vital people trying to realize God's potential for us. On the other hand, if we dream, the fulfillment of those dreams is uncertain, and we are courting disappointment and heartache. Why bother? For in the long run, we, as well as our dreams, will be gone.

A 1989 movie entitled *Casualties of War* addresses this issue of measuring our behavior in this life against eternity. It is based on a true story about a squad of soldiers during the Vietnam war, that time of horror and uncertainty, murder and mayhem. Most of the squad members feel that they have license to do anything because their death is so imminent and their future uncertain. They capture, rape, and murder a young, innocent Vietnamese girl. One member of the squad is a voice of conscience. The man on whom that character is based is still living, now married and a Lutheran. In a conversation with the author of the screenplay, Daniel Lang, here's what he said: "We all figured we might be dead in the next minute, so what difference did it make what we did? But the longer I was over there, the more I became convinced that it was the other way around that counted—that *because* we might not be around much longer, we had to take extra care how we behaved."

That's the bottom line for the Christian. If now is all we have, and the future determines how we behave in the now, then our view of eternity is the ultimate shaping force. What we do now and who we are now will live forever.

Both the now and the future come together with our belief in God, who raised his Son from the dead and who has promised that because he lives, we too shall live. In committing one's life to that Lord who lives now and forever, our fear of the future changes into hope. Whether that hope is fulfilled in this life or the next, we aim for the most grand and glorious design that we can comprehend, being copartners with God in the redemption of His world.

But the Resurrection on that first Easter morning inspired a good deal of fear. In Matthew's account of that event, the word *fear* is mentioned four times in the first ten verses of chapter 28. First, the guards were full of fear. These Roman soldiers must have seen death often. They were prepared to die themselves. Yet, they fell down as though dead. What do you think went through their minds? The two faithful women who came to the tomb to embalm the Lord's body and found instead the risen Christ were just as terrified. Jesus had to reassure them, "Don't be afraid."

As we contemplate that Resurrection, even two thousand years later, it continues to be fearful. If Jesus is not raised from the dead, the future holds little hope, and we ought to be fearful. If it is true, then there are consequences not just eternal, but immediate. The Resurrection is the most revolutionary fact of human history, and being a witness to that Resurrection is the vocation of every believer and the most motivating fact for life now and beyond.

There is no way that you and I can have hope for the future, unless we believe in the God who stands beyond the future and speaks to us about his Resurrection and ours. With that assurance, we can calmly and deliberately and joyfully go about our tentmaking vocations while pursing our number one vocation—proclaiming God's kingdom and working toward its extension.

Without an experience of the Resurrection, we become the frantic people that Merle Shain describes in *Hearts That We Broke Long Ago:* "We just go on dancing faster to contain our fright." When we have met the one who stands beyond the future, we can face all that's ahead with equanimity, middle age, old age, and beyond.

An article in *Time* magazine some time ago examined the perils and promise of middle age. "The young laugh at the way things seem; middle age laughs at the way things are. The young want to dynamite the treasure vaults of life; middle age has learned the combination. The young think they know; middle age knows that no one knows. . . . Before forty, one adds and feeds to gorge the ego; after forty, one subtracts and simplifies to feed the soul."

The future is always uncertain, and it's meant to be. That ingredient adds excitement to life, calls forth our potential, and stretches our aspirations. In one sense, conquering our fear of the future is the key to overcoming a good many of our other fears. It is the litmus test for our faith.

But fear of the future, in particular, provides that catch-all into which any number of our other fears are tossed. The future may hold pain, illness, or financial difficulties. It is the landscape on which those fears of death and hell are focused. Above all, it is unknown and unpredictable.

Compounding a good many of our fears, especially those of illness, pain, and death, is the nagging certainty that we will have to go through them alone. That's the point at which our faith is most pertinent. We *can* trust God, not just in his grand design for our lives and the eventual happy ending to the story, but in his promise that we will have a companion in every circumstance, however fearful. Jesus' last words to his disciples, as recorded in Matthew's gospel, were, "Lo, I am with you always, to the close of the age" (Matt. 28:20, RSV). To the end of our lives, to the end of time, we are not alone, and we can "fear not."

Now for some final words—perhaps the most important words in this whole book. Fear is the handle by which we lay hold on God.

The opposite of faith is fear. Fear makes us withdraw, hide, play it safe. As you look back at the many fears we have examined in these pages, which one is the most crippling or insidious or recurring? Fear of failure or success? Fear of illness or fear of dying? Reread the table of contents and focus on your greatest fear. Believe God wants you to conquer that fear and to prove to you his existence, his love, and his power.

As we said, that very fear is a handle for laying hold on God. When you stop running and face your fear head on with faith, you find God. It is his presence and power that move us beyond our fears—past, present, and future.